PRAISE FOR
mom NEEDS chocolate

Bubble baths are nice, massages are oh so relaxing, and chocolate is necessary to life itself. But there's one more thing that moms need to survive, and that's a daily dose of laughter. *Mom Needs Chocolate* helps meet this need. Whether you have kids at home, or whether you've already raised yours, this book is a fun and fast read for moms of all ages. Motherhood has its rewards, and Debora Coty is one of them.

Martha Bolton
Author of more than 50 books,
including *Didn't My Skin Used to Fit?*

Fabulous, solid ideas from a fine writer.

Sue Buchanan
Author of *I'm Alive and the Doctor's Dead, Friends Through Thick and Thin, Duh-Votions* and *The Bigger the Hair, the Closer to God*

Open this book and pour the contents liberally to sweeten the atmosphere of your home, your head and your heart. Deb knows how to unwrap mom-truth in the most delightful way. *Mom Needs Chocolate* is an invigorating way to treat yourself to a delicious timeout. Go ahead, mom . . . you deserve it!

Patsy Clairmont
Women of Faith speaker
Author, *Catching Fireflies*

Debora definitely knows what it's like to be a mom from those early toddler years right through the teen years. She honestly shares about the trials and frustrations, right along with the joys and rewards of mothering, all with a laugh-out-loud sense of humor. No topic is off-limits. This book will surely entertain you, but more importantly, it will inspire you to be the mother you always hoped to be!

Linda Danis
Author of *365 Things Every New Mom Should Know*

Debora Coty gives us a laugh charge and a life charge that's better than a mocha latte in this delightful read full of real and relatable stories of seeking the joy of the Lord in the trenches of motherhood. Faith-building and fun, witty and wise—get ready for miles of smiles and encouragement that just doesn't quit!

Rhonda Rhea
Speaker, radio personality and humor columnist
Author of *Amusing Grace, Turkey Soup for the Soul—Tastes Just Like Chicken, Who Put the Cat in the Fridge?* and *I'm Dreaming of Some White Chocolate*

I thoroughly enjoyed Debora Coty's *Mom Needs Chocolate*! Her humor and down-to-earth observations make the book not only a great read but also a practical encouragement for women everywhere. Read a chapter a day, and use it as a devotional. I promise you, you will either start your day with a smile, or end with one! And then pick up a copy for a friend!

Holly Wagner
Author of *GodChicks, Daily Steps for GodChicks* and *WarriorChicks*

mom
NEEDS
chocolate

*Hugs, Humor and Hope
for Surviving Motherhood*

Debora M. Coty

Regal

**From Gospel Light
Ventura, California, U.S.A.**

Published by Regal
From Gospel Light
Ventura, California, U.S.A.
www.regalbooks.com
Printed in the U.S.A.

Library of Congress Cataloging-in-Publication Data
Coty, Debora.
Mom needs chocolate : hugs, humor,
and hope for surviving motherhood / Debora Coty.
p. cm.
Includes bibliographical references.
ISBN 978-0-8307-4592-0 (hard cover)
1. Motherhood—Religious aspects—Christianity—Meditations.
2. Motherhood—Anecdotes. 3. Mothers—Religious life—Meditations.
4. Mothers—Religious life—Anecdotes. I. Title.
BV4529.18.C67 2009
242'.6431—dc22
2008047994

2 3 4 5 6 7 8 9 10 / 17 16 15 14 13 12 11 10 09

Rights for publishing this book outside the U.S.A. or in non-English
languages are administered by Gospel Light Worldwide, an international
not-for-profit ministry. For additional information, please visit www.glww.org,
email info@glww.org, or write to Gospel Light Worldwide, 1957
Eastman Avenue, Ventura, CA 93003, U.S.A.

*To my soul sisters who help me out of many a pothole as
we bump along the rocky road of motherhood together:
Cindy, Jan, Cheryl, Gloria, Sandi, Marianne, Brenda, Betty,
Sharon, Denise and Sherry. And to my two wonderful
children without whom I wouldn't be a hot mama:
Matthew Charles and Christina Ruth.
"Rock me a little bit, Mama, just rock me a little bit."*

Contents

Introduction

Who says communion with God must be serious hands-piously-folded periods of prayer on bended knee? Yeesh! As busy moms, who has time for *that*?

I say God is a living creator who breathes His spirit into those devoted to Him in a dynamic, 24/7 relationship. He wants to communicate with us by walking, talking, scraping peanut butter out of the carpet and driving carpool right alongside us.

Whether working within or without our homes, we mothers are consumed by schedules, deadlines, responsibilities, debts—the muck and mire of everyday living. Our spirits yearn to soar but our feet are stuck fast in the mud of daily obligations. We're chronically exhausted and a few fries short of a Happy Meal. Somehow the joy of the Lord checks out on our doorstep.

How, then, can we rejuvenate and redirect our steps toward positive spiritual growth on a day-by-day, diaper-by-diaper level?

Sister, grab a triple chocolate chunk cookie and a cup of hot tea. Come chill with me. Together we'll rediscover God's divinely orchestrated levity of love all around us. And our Father has an amazing sense of humor! He made us, didn't He? Humor is God's catalyst for releasing joy into our souls! He's the master of heaven and mirth, creator of aardvarks, spoonbill platypuses and cowlicks. And He wants us to be filled with His joy, not weighed down by the joy-sucking dully-funks.

Blast those dully-funks, a mother's archenemy!

Oh, c'mon girl, you've been there—that black hole when nothing particularly *bad* is happening, just nothing *good*. Our minds fog, emotions go numb, eyes glaze over; and we move like autotrons in a perpetual state of spiritual dullness.

A busy woman can spend weeks, even years, in the dully-funks, functioning, taking care of her family but NOT experiencing the *fullness* of life Jesus promised to believers in John 10:10: "My purpose is to give life in all its fullness" (*NLT*).

That's what this book's all about—a mom helping other moms trust God to interject His joy as we learn to apply His Word in our crazy, mud-between-the-toes, help-us-Jesus-before-we-tear-our-last-hairs-out *real* lives. A joy-full life really is possible. The joy of hot fudge doesn't even compare with the joy of the Lord!

Don't get me wrong—I'm not denying reality. Bad things happen. Like you, I've paid my dues through disasters, disappointments and depression (which I candidly share in these pages). I've certainly done my share of grousing; but through God's grace, like the psalmist, I've learned, "Oh, the joys of those who put their trust in him!" (Psalm 2:12, *TLB*).

As a plain-talking gal, I don't lollygag around hot topics like enduring marriage, embarrassing children, aging grossfully—er, that is, *gracefully*, maintaining a thankful spirit in an oft-times thankless job (Domestic Queen), loving my neighbor (despite his pizza boxes on my driveway) and straining to hear God's still, small voice above blathering kids, howling pets and snarling traffic.

Hey, I even hit a few girls-only, whisper-behind-the-hand subjects like excessive *boobage* during pregnancy, fashion faux pas, menopause and—gasp!—bodily functions. (Ain't nothin' sacred after poppin' out a baby in front of a dozen pubescent boys in lab coats!)

Above all, I want you to know that it *is* possible to crawl out the other end of the motherhood tunnel spiritually alive and kicking. Draw comfort and strength from God, Godiva and girl-friends. You're not alone in your journey! Keep breathin', sister, and save the last smidge of brownie batter for me!

Love, Deb

My Cups Runneth Over
Pregnancy

A baby is an inestimable blessing and a bother.
MARK TWAIN

As for you, be fruitful and multiply; populate the earth
abundantly and multiply in it.
GENESIS 9:7, *NASB*

There are a few things I've learned while fulfilling the "be fruitful and multiply" mandate.

Pregnancy draws you closer to your spouse. During an emergency stop in our driveway while I tossed my cookies in the grass, my husband, Chuck, tried to comfort me. Soon we were throwing up side by side. It was the most romantic thing he's ever done. Those two brown spots on our lawn were the envy of all my friends.

Childbirth classes are invaluable informational sources. At the country hospital we'd chosen, one young farmer raised his hand the week after we learned about Braxton Hicks false labor contractions. He earnestly addressed the nurse instructor, "Ma'am, my wife's been miserable all week. Could you tell us again about them Briggs and Stratton things?" He was the same strapping fellow who confided the first week, "We ain't ever had any babies, but we've birthed a lot of cows."

The budding momma's swelling belly and the ledge over her innie-turned-outie navel aren't the only evolutions in the body's profile. Average-sized breasts become huge globes that bump into everything. It's like having volleyballs attached to your chest. These alien chest globes take on their own personalities. I called mine the Bobbing Twins, Freddie and Flopsie. I addressed them directly: "Freddie, stop bouncing around or I'm going to fall off this bike," or "Flopsie, you're gonna have to squeeze into this DDD cup—there is no E."

Finally, you're in your ninth month. Ah, but the surprises are not over. After hours of sweating, teeth grinding and PUSHing, you are rewarded with a tiny screaming miracle. The little bugger has a surprisingly strong sucking reflex, and when he latches on, it feels like a vice grip to this incredibly sensitive part of your anatomy. You're awfully glad you did that desensitization with the washcloth beforehand. I once commented to Chuck after performing this unpleasant ritual that rubbing myself with terrycloth made me empathize with that old table he was sanding.

"Hmmm. Yes, dear," he answered, only half listening. I later overheard him inform his sister on the phone, "Debbie uses sandpaper on her chest to get ready for the baby." No wonder his family thinks I'm weird.

Shortly after giving birth, my friend Julia (also a nursing mother) and I decided to take a well-deserved tennis break. Leaving the babies with their daddies, we headed for the courts. The blissful quiet was shattered by a wailing infant in a passing stroller, triggering that mysterious internal milk breaker switch. Julia and I simultaneously clutched our chests like gunshot victims at the incoming flood.

"Stop it, Freddie! Not now, Flopsie!" I pleaded with the Twins as two dark, wet spots appeared in strategic locations on the front of my white tennis shirt. Julia and I mopped ourselves between points with a soggy sweatband, bringing strange new meaning to the term, "bosom buddies."[1]

Son of Man, thank You for the blessing of family and the miracle of babies. Make me more like You because they may end up being like me.

Faith in Action

1. Do you feel that pregnancy drew you closer to your spouse? Why or why not?

2. Which aspects of childbirth will you, like Mary, mother of Jesus, store away and always treasure in your heart? Which ones will you try to forget?

3. Why do you think Jesus referred to himself as the "Son of Man"? (See Matthew 8:20; Mark 9:31; Luke 9:26; John 8:28.)

Note

1. Adapted from "My Cups Runneth Over" by Debora M. Coty, first appearing in *Today's Christian Woman*, November/December 2004 issue. Used by permission.

Greed for Seed . . .
or Chocolate

Piggishness

Laughter is the shortest distance between two people.
VICTOR BORGE

Store up for yourselves treasures in heaven,
where moth and rust do not destroy. . . . For where
your treasure is, there your heart will be also.
MATTHEW 6:20-21, *NIV*

I'll never forget Thelma and Louise, the field mice who moved into our Smoky Mountain cabin when we closed it for winter. I hated to throw out the three cups of birdseed left in the feeder as we packed away the yard doodads until spring, so I left the nearly full birdfeeder inside, propped against the living room wall.

Apparently, our guests let themselves in and spent the winter happily hunkered down in the cabin, busily depositing birdseed in every possible nook and cranny. I can picture them stuffing their bulging cheeks and making trip after trip to store their treasure for future feasts, thinking they'd soon be kicking their little mice feet up on a table and enjoying the good life.

Come spring, we found a full cup of birdseed sequestered in one kitchen drawer and plentiful pawfuls spread throughout every cabinet, closet, and drawer, beneath couch cushions, and even between the bed sheets.

Sadly, we also found the spent bodies of Thelma and Louise keeled over from sheer exhaustion beside the empty bird feeder. Because of their consuming greed for seed, they'd literally worked themselves to death in their futile attempt to store up treasure.

Treasure comes in all shapes and sizes; one's birdseed may be another's money, electronic toys or flashy cars.

Or chocolate.

For me, chocolate summons ravaging, primeval greed, the depth of which is utterly frightening. One piece is never enough. Must have handfuls, basketsful, barrelsful, no—more, more, always more!

Something about that creamy, delicious, delightful stuff causes my usually-controllable gluttony drive to override my good sense and throw all reason out the window. If there's a chocolate bar, I'll eat the whole thing. If there's a bag, I'll empty it. If there's a crate, I'll consume every crumb inside. And I'll do it with full knowledge that I shouldn't, that my derriere is already a sacrificial altar to the Snickers god. Smoke signals billow from the friction generated by my inner thighs when I run.

I don't know why I bother putting chocolate through my lips; I should just smear it directly on my hips.

I try to excuse my greed-driven behavior by blaming the addictive properties of caffeine, but my coffee-guzzling friends don't buy it. I even cited phenylethylamine as my excuse— the hormone stimulated by chocolate that produces that intoxicating, euphoric "love" feeling. What the world needs now is love, sweet love! And as a conscientious citizen of the world, I feel obligated to do my part.

I just read an article about the tremendous health benefits of chocolate (and to the lady nutritionist who wrote it, I say, *You go, girl!*). I'll bite. Literally. I think as women assume greater authoritative positions in the scientific community, there will be more and more evidence unearthed proving that chocolate should be included as one of the basic food groups. I've always considered it a vegetable anyway—it *is* made from cocoa beans!

After a hard day, there's just no better comfort food than a chocolate chip cookie warm from the oven. Or two. Or ten. Slice and bake was a wicked enough temptation, but now Satan himself has created those giant tubs of pre-mixed cookie dough. They're straight from the Fire and Brimstone Bakery. Every day I say, "Get thee behind me, Satan." And he does. It's called cellulite.

Lest you think it's just us fluffy girls who rave the crave, lots of skinny girls agree. Sue Buchanan, author of *I'm Alive and the Doctor's Dead,* is convinced that her consumption of the equivalent of 7 chocolate bars each and every day for the 16 years since she was diagnosed with cancer has been the key to her survival. She purposed to die happy and ended up living happy instead.

In her literary classic, *Just Hand Over the Chocolate and No One Will Get Hurt*, Karen Scalf Linamen says, "Chocolate may be the next best thing to sex, but it can't do miracles. The fact is that there are times when life feels overwhelming and not even a jumbo bag of M&M's will do the trick."

Of course she's right. Chocolate is only a temporary fix. There are certainly times when we must reach for our Bibles instead of Godiva. When anything—including chocolate—

becomes our heart's treasure instead of our relationship with
God, we are missing the biggest treat of all.

> *Everlasting Lord, I want to focus my heart on You*
> *as my greatest treasure. And please help me remember*
> *where I hid all those bite-sized earthly treasures*
> *before they melt!*

Faith in Action

1. What kind of treasure is the Matthew 6 passage re-
   ferring to?

2. What are your greatest treasures—the things your
   heart focuses on most?

3. How do you spend most of your time? How would
   you *prefer* to spend your time? (These are likely your
   treasures.)

Marriage: Desert or Beach?
Marital Harmony

One good husband is worth two good wives; for,
the scarcer things are, the more they're valued.
BENJAMIN FRANKLIN

Marriage is to be held in honor among all.
HEBREWS 13:4, *NASB*

Thinking of my husband warms the cockles of my heart . . .
or could that be heartburn? I'm not really sure what cockles
are, but I think they're like wrinkles, only cockier. And when
heated, they make me do all sorts of silly, sentimental things.
Like repeating "Carl Yastrzemski" (the Boston Red Sox leg-
end) a gazillion times until I can finally say it right, or spending my precious secret stash on surprise tickets to The Who
concert just because he was crazy about them as a teenager
(I, much more cultured, of course, was into The Monkees).

But I wasn't always such a spousal sweetie. My wedding
ring should've been a mood ring. In the early years of our
marriage, my theme verse could have been Proverbs 27:15,
which roughly states that a nagging wife is like a dripping
faucet. The following verse goes on to say that stopping her
is like stopping the wind or trying to hold a handful of oil.
And I could be a slippery little oil slick, let me tell you.

I was determined to "fix" the flaws I found in my mate, whether he wanted to be fixed or not.

Writhing with conviction after a nasty confrontation in 1985, I wrote, "Who, me???" in the margin of my Bible beside Proverbs 21:19: "It is better to live in a desert land than with a contentious and vexing woman" (*NASB*). It's truly perplexing to be vexing. I was only trying to be content, not contentious; to bask in the sun on the beach, not wither in the desert. The *NIV* translation uses the terms "quarrelsome" and "ill-tempered." Yikes. Could those awful words describe me?

Poor Solomon must have had more than a few dripping faucets amongst his thousand or so wives to write about us so succinctly. (The man must've been a glutton for punishment to *want* more than one wife! Can you imagine the hormones zinging off the walls of that harem?)

Light finally dawned with Proverbs 10:19: "When there are many words, transgression is unavoidable, but he who restrains his lips is wise" (*NASB*).

What a novel concept for me! Keep my wise and helpful suggestions for spousal improvement to myself? Why, I was sure the Master Potter couldn't mold my husband into a vessel of excellence without my clay-stained fingers creeping up from beneath the table to help.

But to my surprise, when I backed off, my husband's unique qualities were much clearer and I could better appreciate the fine, godly man with whom I'd been blessed. (Sort of like restraining your fingers from the batter so you can later enjoy more delicious brownies warm from the oven.)

It took a few more years of diligent effort for me to learn to *honor* my husband by putting Proverbs 15:1 into practice: "A gentle answer turns away wrath, but a harsh word stirs up anger" (*NASB*). What a difference it made in our marital relationship when I managed to swallow those harsh words before they incited a skirmish, undermined our mutual trust in one another and eroded our sense of intimacy.

Hurtful words are like daggers; the wounds they inflict bleed and fester and require a long time to heal.

Some wounds never do.

No one said it's easy to dam the flow of angry words that threaten to gush out when we disagree. But it *is* possible in the Holy Spirit's power and well worth the prayerful effort if I choose to honor the God-ordained institution of marriage and the only one with whom I wish to be institutionalized.

Love Divine, throughout this entire day, help me see my cellmate—er, that is, marriage partner—through Your loving eyes.

Faith in Action

1. If you're married, what do you feel when you think of your husband? (Your answer will probably be a mixed bag of emotions; try to name them.)

2. How do you compare with the woman described in Proverbs 27:15? (A dripping faucet; as stoppable as the wind; and as slippery as a handful of oil.)

3. Name two practical ways you can begin to practice Proverbs 15:1 with your cellmate, er, that is, your marriage partner.

The Perfect Gift
Spiritual Gifts

Every mother is like Moses. She does not enter the promised land.
She prepares a world she will not see.
POPE PAUL VI

God has also given each of us different gifts to use. . . .
If we can serve others, we should serve. If we can teach, we should teach.
If we can encourage others, we should encourage them. . . .
If we are good to others, we should do it cheerfully.
ROMANS 12:6-8, *CEV*

Scribbled beside the Romans 12 passage in my Bible are the words, *I am unique; I am needed!* Pretty cool conclusion considering the number of years and brain cells I have spent trying to figure out what my spiritual gift is. During my exhaustive quest, at least I've discovered what it's *not*.

My friend Denise has the gifts of service and hospitality. She hosts our Wednesday night Bible study week after week, year after year. Not only does she rush home from work to cook dinner and feed her family, clean house and prepare scrumptious refreshments, but she does it *cheerfully*. AACK! She always has a spread of fresh fruit, something salty with dip(s) and homemade sweet treats with a myriad of flavored coffees, all served on her best china.

When we arrive, the kitchen is spotless, scented candles are burning, lights are low for ambiance and Denise greets us with a big smile and warm hug. For every possible occasion, Denise presents each of us with adorable gifts (ceramic Easter bunnies filled with chocolate eggs, Pilgrim figurines, stuffed Groundhog's Day rodents—you get the picture).

I think the friendship between Denise and me is made in heaven; she's a joyful giver and I'm an exuberant taker.

When I host groups, I serve a bag of chips, canned bean dip and low-carb soda (that's low *carbonation* because the three-week-old 2-liter bottle cap wasn't screwed on tightly). My guests consider themselves lucky if cups are anywhere in sight (otherwise they have to swig out of the same flat soda bottle) and someone usually pulls me aside to discreetly report doggie-doo lurking in a corner. The only present my guests leave with is a coating of cat hair on their derrieres.

Okay, so I obviously don't have the gift of hospitality.

For a long time, I thought spectating was my special talent, but our pastor gently pointed out that bench warming was not a spiritual gift. He had this weird idea about getting *involved* instead of appreciating the work of others from my safe seat in the congregation. But what would all the doers of the world do without us spectators? They'd have no one to cheer them on!

One attribute I've developed fully is *worry*. I'm a worrier of the highest order, a gold medal champion. I truly believe there's tremendous benefit in diligently building those molehills into mountains. It keeps the blood pumping, the stomach acids churning and those bothersome nails down to a practical nub.

Alas, after scouring the Romans 12, Ephesians 4, and 1 Corinthians 12 passages about spiritual gifts, I didn't see worry among them. Bummer.

Let's see, then, what gift *do* I have? Teaching? My husband and I led a junior high Bible study for three years; one girl got pregnant, another got arrested for shoplifting and two boys dropped out of school. We still get calls from another resourceful lad between jail sentences.

Prophecy? The future's a fog to me. I don't even know what I'm fixing for dinner tonight, and it's 5:00 P.M. Guess that one's out. Miracles? God arranges mini-miracles in my life every single day (I call them His amazing grace notes), but I can't say I have the gift of miracles. Been praying for my bum knee for years and it still squeaks.

Encouragement? Hmmm. Now this one I *can* do! There are so many different ways to encourage—a genuine smile, a listening ear, a compassionate hug. And God gave me lips, ears and arms that work just swell. He must have known this was my special gift all along. Of course *I'm* the one encouraged most when I encourage others, so it's a win-win situation.

Bestower of perfect gifts, thank You for the special talents and abilities You've given each of us to emulate and glorify You. Help me unwrap and enjoy my unique gifts today!

Faith in Action

1. List three special talents God has given you (come on now, I *know* you can come up with at least three!)

2. Read Ephesians 4:11-12, 1 Corinthians 12:8-10 and 1 Peter 4:8-11. Do you agree that your special combination of gifts is unique? Why or why not?

3. What is your greatest spiritual gift? How are you currently using it for God's glory?

I'm Terribly Sorry . . . Sort of

Repentance

> *Joy is God living in the marrow of your bones.*
> BARBARA JOHNSON

> *Do something to show that you have really given up your sins.*
> MATTHEW 3:8, *CEV*

I was only gone for 10 seconds. When I returned from the kitchen, clutching a napkin, the last half of my sandwich had disappeared from my plate. A telltale trail of crumbs led behind the couch.

"FENWAY! What have you done with my lunch?"

Only a stubby wagging tail was visible as my toy poodle (his name a testimonial to my husband, the die-hard Boston Red Sox fan) worked busily on his forbidden bounty.

"Get your little thieving self over here *right now!*" I bellowed.

Two liquid brown eyes peered at me around the side of the couch.

"I mean it, Fenway; drop the loot and come here, you naughty dog!"

He must have realized I was angry, because he assumed the "Aren't I adorable?" pose that usually melts my heart. A speck of onion bread clung to his furry chin.

The judge and jury found him guilty as charged and threw him into the brig. Social butterfly that he is, solitary confinement is the only punishment that speaks to him, so his sentence was 15 minutes in the bathroom to mull over his crime.

From the wailing, yipping, and howling that ensued, you'd think I had beat him with a crowbar. After 10 minutes, I started feeling badly for the poor puppy. He certainly sounded repentant. He was sorry he'd sinned; I could hear it in his mournful voice. Maybe he couldn't help himself. Maybe it was an innate primal urge. I shouldn't punish a dog for being a dog, should I?

I opened the bathroom door and knelt with my arms stretched wide to receive my contrite canine. He dashed out of his prison and ran right past me, through the kitchen, through the living room and behind the couch to finish his sandwich.

I, too, often find myself in the paradox of insincere repentance. My head knows it was wrong to speak critically of that annoying person, and my heart asks my heavenly Father for forgiveness, but my mouth turns around and does it again at the next opportunity. I may wail and yip and howl about being repentant, but if I repeat the offense, it was all just noise. The "sorry" didn't take.

God speaks of second chances in the parable of the barren fig tree in Luke 13:6-9. When the landowner wants to destroy the figless fig tree, the caretaker steps in and promises to personally nurture the little tree toward change if it's given just one more chance. In the same way, God generously gives us second chances to sincerely repent when we sin. He doesn't want that sin blocking our fellowship with Him.

As animal trainers have shown us, even self-centered, tummy-driven Fenway can alter his behavior if he's motivated enough. How much more can we, children of the King, choose to reflect genuine repentance by changing our actions to reflect our father's heart?

Dear "Rock that is Higher than I" [Psalm 61:2, KJV], help me prove that I'm truly sorry for my sins by changing my behavior. And in the meantime, mightn't You send me another turkey and cheese on onion bread?

Faith in Action

1. Do you find it difficult to *meaningfully* say "I'm sorry"? Many of us do; why do you think that is?

2. After reading Jesus' parable in Luke 13:6-9, describe a second chance God has given you during the last week. Now recount a second chance you've offered to one of your children.

3. Are there any sins in your life of which you have not truly repented? (That means you have shown you're sorry by changing your behavior.)

Does Growing Mold Count as Gardening?

Remembrance

Humor is a powerful salve for the skinned knees of the spirit.
DEBORA M. COTY

*The earth produced all kinds of vegetation. God looked
at what he had done, and it was good.*
GENESIS 1:12, *CEV*

Ah, the joys of gardening—there's nothing like the aroma of fresh toadstools and the feel of earthworms squiggling between your toes! I suppose growing green fuzzy things in my refrigerator doesn't really mean I have a green thumb. My gardening thumb is actually a dingy shade of brown (like the stuff growing on my bathroom tile).

Despite my anemic horticultural skills, I love to experience the seasons in my garden. I feel God's warm heartbeat through the perfect rhythm of His creation, reflecting seasons of my own life—cyclic phases of dormancy, sprouting, growth, blooming, struggle, death and, miraculously, new life.

Ten years ago, I started a memory garden—nothing formal, really, just an area of my yard where special plants remind me of special people. When my beloved grandmother passed away at Christmastime, my mother insisted I take an enormous poinsettia sent in condolence. My grandmother was a colorful woman and the crimson poinsettia seemed fittingly symbolic of her life. I planted it in a secluded spot in my backyard; tending to it made me feel close to her and brought solace to my hollow heart.

When my aunt died the following year, I planted the peace lily I inherited from her funeral near the poinsettia. My aunt was a lovely, quiet woman whose legacy was serenity and dignity—qualities portrayed by the lily. The graceful plant still brings a smile to my face in fond remembrance.

The weeds surrounding the poinsettia and lily (hey, I never said I was a *real* gardener!) remind me to pray for my cousins, especially Howard, who rolled me down the rocky hill in a metal barrel as a child. Man, it hurt! Maybe my memory garden works a little *too* well.

My ginger plant border is a testimonial to God's grace and the miracle of forgiveness. Twenty years ago, I had a falling-out with my then best friend, Tessa. Our husbands were coworkers, and Tessa and I, nearly inseparable, shared the joys and challenges of first-time motherhood.

When Tessa's husband was promoted, an element of jealousy was partially responsible for a terrible miscommunication between us, resulting in a complete breach of our relationship. Tessa moved out of state. For 15 years, my guilt-motivated prayers lifted her up to the Lord.

Then one Sunday, to my utter astonishment, I spotted Tessa across our church sanctuary. With a pounding heart and a prayer for guidance, I approached her. She'd unknowingly attended my church because it was near her mother's home, Tessa's temporary respite since a bitter divorce. She invited me over for tea.

God's presence was strong during that visit, and we reconciled, tearfully forgiving each other and praying together in humble gratefulness for a friendship restored. A huge cinderblock lifted off my shoulders. As I was leaving, I admired a ginger plant growing in the yard. Tessa reached down and plucked a tiny twig sprouting a few limp roots and handed it to me with a hug.

Tessa soon moved away, but the twig has since grown 100-fold into a mighty hedge. To me, it depicts God's immutable power and the hope of reconciliation in our lives. When I pray for a friend's estranged father or another's prodigal daughter, I sit in the shade of the towering ginger plant and *know* that God can indeed knit torn relationships back together.

Three years ago, we were devastated to learn that the 20-year-old daughter of dear friends had been killed. Lisa and my children had been friends since birth. Searching for a fitting memorial, I purchased a bleeding heart vine for Lisa's parents and one for myself, its delicate red and white blossoms representing our grief at the loss of one so young and beautiful, but also joy that Christ's bleeding heart had ensured that we would see Lisa again in heaven one day.

Lisa's mother planted her vine in a sunny corner by the house, where it has branched out, as if Lisa herself were encircling her family with arms of love. My bleeding heart vine entwines a tree in my memory garden and constantly evokes gratitude for a hope-filled future through Christ.

Even if all you've ever grown is algae on your shower drain, consider starting a memory garden. We, too, grow abundantly from God's little horti-miracles that nurture *us* and give back so much more than the effort they take.

Master Gardener, nurture my spiritual growth,
prune me when necessary and make me bloom
through Your loving care. Thank You for the precious
people that have touched my life, and use their memories
to inspire me to become more like You.

Faith in Action

1. Describe any items or areas in your home that serve as a memorial to special people who have touched your life.

2. Which person(s) from your past had the most impact on your life?

3. How do you feel about gardening and growing things? Have you ever considered allowing God's little horti-miracles to minister to you?

Didn't that Verse Say "Loathe Your Neighbor"?

Loving Our Enemies

The heart that loves is always young.
GREEK PROVERB

Love your enemies and pray for anyone who mistreats you.
Then you will be acting like your Father in heaven.
MATTHEW 5:44-45, CEV

Have you ever met someone who lived by the Nedlog Rule? Followers of the Nedlog Rule believe, "Don't do for others because they don't do for you!" Nedlog would be the Golden Rule backwards (you know, the one that says, "Do unto others as you would have them do unto you").

I first met Helene and her husband, Rodney, at a neighborhood Bible study. They were in the process of building an enormous home in our subdivision (twice as large as mine, but who's measuring?) and wanted to get to know the neighbors. Rodney was friendly and outgoing, but Helene was a sullen non-mingler. As weeks passed, Helene's critical comments estranged her from everyone. I, too, groaned inwardly whenever I arrived late and found the only open chair next to Helene.

Somehow, she latched on to me as her confidante and began seeking me out at church and community events. After moving into her mansion, Helene frequently invited me to go shopping and didn't seem put off by my chronic declines necessitated by the needs of my brood. Without children or a job of her own, Helene was unable to grasp the fact that I was drowning in the sea of motherhood, and she phoned me three to five times daily.

Hints fell on deaf ears. Legitimate excuses didn't work. But I knew she had no friends and I just couldn't bring myself to add to her rejection.

Then she began stalking me.

If I didn't pick up the phone when she called (hooray for caller ID!), she'd leave a message for me to return her call ASAP. If I didn't hurriedly close the garage door and shut all the curtains, the next terse message would freak me out. "I just drove by your house and saw your car. I know you're home. Why aren't you returning my call?"

I felt like a fugitive in my own home.

My kids became spies, peeking through the front blinds. "The crazy lady's driving by the house again, Mom!" I ducked when I saw her coming, hid inside bathroom stalls at church, dove behind pyramids of canned beans at the grocery store and rerouted my exercise walk to avoid her street.

When her first child arrived, Helene became occupied with mothering but still kept in touch. One day, she informed me that Rodney had just spent several hundred dollars sprucing up their lawn and flowerbeds so they would win the neighborhood yard judging contest. As longtime coordinator for this event, my job was to drive the master gardener judges around the neighborhood, tally votes and announce the winners. I cringed to think that her call might be meant to sway the results.

Observing Helene's yard on the day of the contest, one judge remarked, "That one's got a long way to go." The day the winners were posted, I received an irate call from Helene, demanding to know why her house hadn't won. I spared her the judge's criticism. During the following weeks, Helene spread rumors that the contest was rigged, that Debbie Coty was grossly unfair and only her best friends won.

My heart hardened against Helene. I no longer worried about her feelings.

Communication dissolved between us for the next two years. I heard that shortly after their second child was born, Rodney left Helene. I'm ashamed to admit that my first thought was, "Who can blame him?"

But a peculiar thing happened. God gradually transformed my perspective. I started walking past Helene's house again. As I gazed at the impenetrable walls of her lonely castle, my heart softened. I sensed her pain and surprisingly, I cared. I began lifting her up in prayer—her shattered marriage, her single parenting, her solitary existence.

Within a few weeks, Helene tentatively appeared at my door trick-or-treating with her kids. She looked like she might run away. I smiled. Then she smiled. We connected. Later, I was able to honestly cry with her and blanket her with God's comforting embrace as she spilled out her despair. My daughter, observing the transformation, remarked, "Wow—hasn't that lady changed?"

But I know it was me that changed.

Something miraculous happens when we pray for our enemies. A supernatural scalpel filets us open for God to reach inside and perform a heart transplant. It's one of the most Christ-like things we can do. Jesus prayed for His murderers even as He hung on the cross.

Sometimes prayer is all it takes to transform loathing into loving.

Master Restorer, the next time I'm tempted to apply the Nedlog Rule, paint my perspective golden.

Faith in Action

1. Does any particular "enemy" come to mind when you read Matthew 5:44-45?

2. Relate three actions or attitudes that cause your heart to harden against people. Can you visualize any specific people toward whom you've become hardened?

3. Have you considered praying for these people and allowing God's supernatural scalpel to perform a heart transplant in you? Will you commit to start today?

8

An Uncommon Tail
Motivation

If you don't have a sense of humor,
you probably don't have any sense at all.
AUTHOR UNKNOWN

Ask the animals, and they will teach you.
JOB 12:7, *NIV*

Rodents. The word alone tingles many a mom's spine. Nay, not me! My household is into critters, and I've found that God often uses the simplicity and honesty of even his lowliest creatures to speak to my heart.

One memorable sensei was a hamster that could lift more weight than Schwarzenegger—per ounce of body density—to achieve her goal of freedom. No matter how many phone books or dictionaries were piled atop her enclosure (I'm talking up to 60 times her body weight), she would wedge herself on top of her exercise wheel and press her spindly little legs against the ceiling of her cage, working ceaselessly to slide that lid the quarter inch necessary to escape.

During her surprise nocturnal visits that inevitably followed, I often thought, as I leapt from my violated bed, screeching loud enough to wake Lazarus, that I should be so motivated to attain my goals. Nothing could stop that furry ball of determination. Chuck thought that she was demon-possessed, but I felt sure it was pure female passion.

Sometimes it's hard to tell the difference.

I'm a quitter by nature. I hate to admit it, but there it is. In my pre-maternal days, if something wasn't going right or required an inordinate amount of effort, I'd just shrug and turn my attention elsewhere. But when children came along, I could hardly ignore my daughter when she refused to eat, or let my son run out in the road because I was tired of correcting him for the thousandth time. I had to grit my teeth and do again and again whatever was necessary to achieve the ultimate goal of my kids living through their childhood.

It's tempting to pray for elimination of the nuisances and obstacles in our lives, but we must realize that the creek would never dance if God removed the rocks. It helps to remember 1 Peter 1:6-7: "Be truly glad! There is wonderful joy ahead, even though the going is rough for a while down here. These trials are only to test your faith" (*TLB*).

In recent years, I've had to learn perseverance in my writing career. With enough rejection slips to wallpaper a ballroom, I've taken a clue from my rodent mentor and have just kept pushing on that lid to my cage. I figure that just as jockeys have to put up with horse poo as a vocational hazard, I must step over the piles of rejection notices, wipe the nasty off my boots and keep going.

But how do we find motivation to keep going when our reserves are drained? Well, a Tootsie Roll wouldn't hurt. Or a Baby Ruth. Or one of those delightfully unpronounceable French chocolates wrapped in crinkly gold foil . . . okay, okay. My mind is refocusing, and I've stopped drooling.

Seriously, sisters, that's exactly what we need: focus. (You thought I was going to say chocolate, didn't you?) If we redirect our attention and energies to the one true source of strength, our heavenly Father will provide His abundant power to persevere.

How do we tap into this vital source of infinite motivation? Through reading and meditating on Scripture (so He can talk to us), earnest prayer (so we can talk back), and by surrounding ourselves with stimuli that focuses on God. You've already got a great start by reading this book! Remember, we become what we think about most.

I'm happy to report that the highly-motivated hamster did achieve her goal of freedom. One day she escaped and never came back. I like to picture her running with wild abandon through a flower-dotted field, her fur blowing in the warm breeze and a smile on her ecstatic little face.

So when you're tempted to give up *your* fight, remember this little poster child of sheer determination. And crank out a few squats.

Come thou fount of every blessing, fill my dry tanks with Your invigorating streams of living water. And goose me over all the piles of horse poo in my path.

Faith in Action

1. What area of your life requires the most perseverance right now?

2. According to 1 Peter 1:6, what are two ways we can draw strength to persevere?

3. Consider your schedule and list one thing you can do each day to connect to God's abundant power source.

9

Even Moses Started Out as a Basket Case

Forgiveness

*In automobile terms, the child supplies the power
but the parents have to do the steering.*
BENJAMIN SPOCK

*Jesus said, "Let the children come to me, and don't try to stop them!
People who are like these children belong to God's kingdom."*
MATTHEW 19:14, CEV

"Now, how did he *do* that?" I asked my 22-month-old son's empty stroller, the seatbelt buckled around . . . air.

"Matthew? Baby Houdini? The game's over; come out!" I called softly, trying not to draw attention to myself as I looked under, around and through the racks of blouses I had been perusing. I already felt out of place, having entered the mall's most upscale boutique on a whim. It was a foreign land compared to my usual discount department store haunts.

I crawled to an adjoining display of evening dresses on my hands and knees. "Enough is enough, Matthew," I hissed through hair hanging over my face. "Get out of there right now!"

"May I help you, madam?" asked a silken voice from above.

"Uh—no, thanks. I'm just looking for something I've lost."

"And what exactly might that be?" she cooed in a voice dripping with honey. "Perhaps I could be of assistance." A nametag proclaiming *Ms. Hightower, Manager* (name changed to protect the snooty) dropped into my worm's eye view on the lapel of the designer-suited woman as she attempted to lower herself to my level—as if that were possible.

I scrambled to my feet, tugging my sweatshirt over K-Mart jeans. "Well, it's not exactly some*thing*, it's more like some*one*—"

At that moment, we were interrupted by a roar of laughter from a group of mall shoppers gathered at the store entrance, pointing to the large display window where mannequins were posed in various positions to display the store's finery. Drawing the most attention at the moment was the blonde mannequin seated on the floor with her arms raised in a gesture of frozen festivity. Colored stockings were stretched from the tip of each finger to form an intricate web of rainbow-hued hosiery extending to the ceiling.

There, seated in her statuesque lap, with his chubby little arm wrapped around her plastic neck, was my missing son. Giggling gleefully, Matthew smashed his cookie against her painted lips and jostled her curly wig over one glassy eye.

As I dived for the back of the display window, I glimpsed Ms. Hightower's pale face, her perfectly waxed eyebrows arching in horror, the faux blush on her cheeks distinct round splotches like strawberries in a bowl of cream.

The window's entrance was a sliding panel that was locked in place, leaving a space just wide enough for an inquisitive toddler to squeeze through. "Matthew, come to Mommy!" I called through the hole. His adoring audience guffawed as he poked his new friend and responded, "Ooh Mommy! Look—pretty lady!"

Realizing that a toddler with groupies was not going to be reasonable, I shoved my arm into the opening and groped blindly for my prodigal son. He and his fans only laughed harder as my flailing upper extremity assaulted the pretty lady, whacking her in the face and sending her blonde wig flying.

As Matthew shifted positions, I lunged and managed to snag the toe of his sneaker. I began reeling him in, inch by inch. *Zing! Pang! Ptewie!* The myriad of colored hose attached to the mannequin's fingers popped loose from the ceiling like rogue gunshots as Matthew dragged the petrified lady along for the ride, upending two other mannequins before I managed to wedge his squirming body through the narrow opening. Matthew emerged from battle clutching a plastic arm bearing the remnants of once-lovely stockings—like shredded flags after a war.

I hastily handed the dismembered appendage to an open-mouthed Ms. Hightower, muttered a mortified, "I'm so sorry," and fled the crime scene with Matthew howling in his getaway stroller.

I felt the fury roil inside like a pot about to boil over. "You're a *bad* boy, Matthew! How could you do this to me? You're a *bad, bad* boy!" As I spat the angry words at my son, I suddenly realized how many times I, too, must've embarrassed my heavenly Father that day by my bad behavior: those heated words with my husband over breakfast, cutting off that pushy driver, pocketing the extra dollar of change the clerk had mistakenly given me. But God loved me anyway. My poor choices didn't make me *bad* in God's eyes . . . only in need of forgiveness.

I stopped the stroller and got down on my knees, face-to-face with my sniffling toddler. "Mommy made a mistake, little buddy. You're not a *bad* boy. You just do naughty things sometimes. So do I. But we forgive and love each other anyway. Just like God does."

Beloved Papa God, thank You for loving me unconditionally. Help me teach by example Your forgiveness and mercy to those You've entrusted to my care.

Faith in Action

1. Describe a time when your child embarrassed you in public (I know there are thousands to choose from, but please name only one).

2. Do you, like many mothers, struggle with forgiving your child when he or she overwhelms you with bad behavior?

3. Name two instances when you probably embarrassed your heavenly Father with your less-than-sterling behavior. How does it feel to know you're forgiven?

Under Control
God's Omnipotence

Humor is God's weapon against worry, anxiety and fear.
OLD ADAGE

How well he understands us and knows what is best for us at all times.
EPHESIANS 1:8, *TLB*

There's no greater feeling of helplessness than when everything goes wrong and you feel totally out of control. Your frustration level hits red alert and you wonder if your guardian angel is tanning her wings in Bermuda.

I was waiting to board a flight in Chicago when a tsunami of nausea crashed over me. *Uh oh,* I thought. *Ignore it and it'll go away.* An after-wave hit, and then another. The first group of passengers was called to board the plane. *Do I have time for the bathroom? Yes—no—oh, no! It's that dreaded middle RHEA sister of the infamous trio, PyorRHEA, DiarRHEA, and GonorRHEA!*

I painstakingly passed the ticket counter and tiptoed down the long corridor to the plane. It was sheer torture. With every step that Rhea sister became more insistent on an immediate visit. I was facing the flight attendant when I knew with no uncertainty that I had to go NOW.

"I . . . I'm going to be sick," I whisper-screamed, turning to flee up the crowded corridor like a salmon struggling upstream. Breaking free, I galloped past the startled ticket-taker into the terminal, calling over my shoulder, "Please hold—plane—sick—be right back!"

"You'd better hurry!" Her voice floated after me, "I can't hold it very long!"

"You're telling me!" I croaked.

Tethered to the ladies' room, I helplessly listened to the cotton-candy loudspeaker voice crooning the last call for my flight. Near tears, I choked down a fistful of Imodium and dashed for the gate, frantically praying, *Make it stop, Lord! You calmed the stormy sea; please quell my stormy guts.*

I burst through the plane door panting and sweaty. As I bumped my rolling carry-on down the center aisle, every eye stared. They knew. Worse yet, I knew they knew.

The plane taxied and lifted off, pressure shifting my sphincter muscles into high gear. I'm positive that Moses prayed no more passionately at the Red Sea. But praise our merciful Lord, He heard my pleas, and by mid-flight, the waters parted.

A friendly tip about traveling: Always pack extra underwear. In your purse. Tell the search guys you're a rap star and it's a do-rag. Act *totally* cool as you explain this.

My friend Drina saves her holey, elastic-challenged panties for vacations. She wears them once with a pad, again without and then trashes them, lightening her luggage for more souvenirs. Great idea!

But beware of underpants with anemic elastic. I once wore a pair to work at the rehab center (I'm an occupational therapist when I'm not writing or teaching piano or wiping noses or cooking or chauffeuring). Mid-morning, something started feeling odd down south. I glanced in a mirror and saw the outline of my panties creeping down my pants legs.

Ducking into a storage room, I stuck my hand down the back of my trousers to retrieve the drooping drawers when suddenly the door was yanked open by a male physical therapist. His teeth clattered as they hit the floor. Scarred for life, he was. At the company Christmas party the following month, he presented me with a 3-pack of brand-new, mighty-tighty Fruit of the Looms.

When these seemingly out-of-control things happen, we can laugh, cry, die of embarrassment or praise the Lord because we know He truly is still in control. I do all of the above . . . and sing a little song I wrote:

Chorus (repeat with gusto after each verse):

You've got it under control, Lord.
You've got it under control.
When life gets out of hand, just help me understand
You've got it under control.

Verses (snap fingers on the offbeat and wag head
side to side):

I woke up at eight, that old alarm didn't sound;
The kids were late for school and it's the fourth
      time around.
I'm driving back home and see the homework
      smiling at me . . . from the seat.
Sometimes motherhood ain't all it's cracked
      up to be.

I'm standing at the checkout in the gro-ce-ry store;
The bill's a hundred dollars like it was the week before;

Got company coming, there's everything here you
    could eat . . .
        except meat!
And then the checkbook's gone and all I've got's
    a dollar on me.

I rush home from work, got a thousand things to do.
My daughter stands before me with her eyes
    a'shining blue;
Says "Mommy, won't you play with me?" and
    throws her little arms around my neck.
What the heck?
Guess the dishes can wait and the dog won't starve
    before I get back.

*Omnipotent Father, sometimes I live in the state of Florida,
sometimes in the state of panic. Help me remember, even in
those crazy, chaotic moments, that You are in control.*

Faith in Action

1. What is your typical reaction when out-of-control things happen?

2. In light of Ephesians 1:8, do you think God is surprised at your response?

3. Name one thing you vow to do differently next time things seem out of control. (Examples: call for help in the form of a quickie prayer; stop and count five blessings while your blood pressure descends; cease beating your head with your purse before concussion occurs.)

Duty Doesn't Call, It Screams

Balancing Work and Family

*It's easy for a mom to hear herself talking;
she just has to listen to her four-year-old.*
AUTHOR UNKNOWN

*She is clothed in fine linen and purple. . . . she makes linen garments
and sells them, and supplies the merchants with sashes. She is clothed
with strength and dignity; she can laugh at the days to come.*
PROVERBS 31:22, 24-25, *NIV*

The Proverbs 31 woman is our example of a godly woman who has her life in balance. She's careful of her appearance, maintains her sense of humor and is strong and industrious, creating and selling goods in the marketplace.

My problem in looking for balance is that I tend to take "industrious" to the far end of the spectrum. I'm productive to a fault. I don't know when to quit. More (unfortunately) is neither better nor godlier. Like me, many moms struggle to find the balance between work and family.

My daughter's eyes pierced the back of my skull as I sat at my computer tapping away. "I *hate* that computer," she muttered. Startled, I turned to find her standing in the doorway, arms crossed and lower lip protruding.

"You'd rather spend time with that machine than with me," she pouted.

Her words cut like a serrated knife. With a pang of guilt, I realized I'd answered her plea for mommy time with, "Give me just 10 minutes," which had turned into 30, then an hour, then two.

I wonder what the Proverbs 31 woman did with her kids while she cut, sewed and marketed those linen garments.

I've always struggled with putting *things* ahead of *people*. Productivity is my tyrannical master, driving me to do, do, do. But all that incessant *do* only results in a severe case of calendar constipation. My resolve to chill is constantly over-powered by that inner force urging me to "just finish this," or "make a little headway" on that.

People sometimes comment how sweet it is that my daughter holds my hand as we walk through the house to-gether. What they don't know is that she's hanging on with a calculated death grip because she knows if she lets go, I'll get busy elsewhere. The only way to get me to her desired destination is to lead me on a leash. Otherwise, everything I walk past screams my name to be cleaned, adjusted, put away, fixed or attended to in some sidetracking manner.

I'm plagued by that blasted Time Contortion Contin-uum.[1] The TCC is that strange phenomenon caused by the contortion of all that time you thought you had but which has mysteriously vanished. It plays out like this: the earlier you get up, the later you are.

As an early riser (my internal rooster crows precisely at 5:40 every morning), I have a false sense of security about scheduled events. Of course I can make it to an 8:00 A.M. appointment on time. How could I *not* with all that time to spare?

But somehow the more time I have the more tasks I find to fill it. My young kids had a way of filling the time with last-minute diaper changes, juice spills and forgotten home-work. But now that they're independent, I manage to find plenty of things that simply must be done before leaving the house. Empty the dishwasher, iron a few shirts, make out a grocery list, mop the bathroom, answer my email . . . any one of these activities could easily be accomplished in the 15 spare minutes I have; but no, I must do them *all*.

And then, as brilliant a multi-tasker as I fancy myself, my ears seem to short-circuit when my attention is divided among a myriad of tasks. I miss hearing all sorts of crucial things: what time to pick up my husband from the car repair shop; how many friends my kids invited over for dinner; the date and time of the rescheduled meeting with the teacher. Of course, I earnestly insist that I was never told this infor-mation in the first place, but the bottom line is that my fam-ily suffers because I'm too scattered to focus.

I read somewhere that when you're stressed, the ante-rior brain constricts and blood flow is reduced to the audi-tory organs. You truly don't hear as well. I'll buy it. Sounds like a good excuse to me.

Another hair-ripping element of the TCC is the way time drags on sleepless nights while you're tossing in a sea of bed sheets; but time zips by in hyper-drive when com-pany's coming and the full gravy boat hits the linoleum. I think there's an angel in heaven with a warped sense of hu-mor manning the TCC joystick:

"Cool! Let's delete 10 more minutes and watch that mop fly like greased lightning!"

"Whoa—back up the sleep train . . . I bet I can squeeze in an extra half hour between 2:00 and 3:00 A.M.! Watch her flopping around in that bed—you go, girl! You need the exercise!"

Teach me when to quit, Lord. My family is just too costly
to sacrifice in the name of productivity. Help me remem-
ber that people are always more important than things.

Faith in Action

1. Read Proverbs 31; does the "perfect" woman sound as busy as you are?

2. How do you balance busyness and family? Are you consistently able to put people above things? Do you feel you need help in this area?

3. In what ways does the TCC (Time Contortion Continuum) drive you batty?

Note

1. The Time Contortion Continuum is another original Coty near-fact of science.

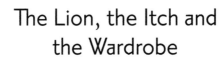

The Lion, the Itch and the Wardrobe

Depression

I tried to think deeply, but I just couldn't pull it off.
ANDIE HARDEE, AGE 15

*I will give you a new heart and put a new spirit in you; I will remove
from you your heart of stone and give you a heart of flesh.*
EZEKIEL 36:26, *NIV*

Depression is not funny. But, like most serious situations in life, finding the slim thread of submerged humor is often essential in weaving the intricate fabric of healing.

One crisp fall morning, I'd taken time off from work for a dental appointment, only to be told that extensive—and expensive—work was needed. How could things get worse? For long months, I'd been dealing with my husband's flat-on-his-back illness and our dire financial straits due to the disappearance of his straight commission income. Intimacy between us had evaporated. Loneliness and endless stress took their toll. Depression crept in, graying my world. I felt numb, void of all feeling. Laughter became a distant memory.

Sometimes I cried out to God. Sometimes I just cried. My faith had endured many trials, but this time, my pleas for help seemed to bounce off the ceiling. My prayer life had become as brittle and shriveled as a dry fallen leaf.

Slumping in my car in the dentist's parking lot, my mood was scraping bottom. With my lunch hour approaching, I considered visiting the small zoo nearby. *Maybe the animals will give me a lift,* I thought, woodenly cranking the car.

There were few people milling about as I crested the hill leading to the lion enclosures. I noticed a couple with two young children standing in front of the female lions' cage as I approached. I'd been there only a few seconds when suddenly one of two enormous tawny females lounging lackadaisically jumped to her feet and her steely eyes zeroed in on mine. A long, low growl rolled from her throat as she kept her vision glued to me and paced at the front of the cage.

The wide-eyed boy holding his father's hand said, "I don't think that lion likes you, lady," as I smiled nervously and took a small step backward. Without warning, the angry lioness lunged forward, roaring resoundingly and baring sharp teeth as she thrust one huge clawed paw between the iron bars in my direction.

We all took a giant step backward at that, and faces in the crowd turned to stare at me as the angry lioness unleashed her ferocious attempts to rip me to shreds. "What did you do to make her so mad?" asked the little girl.

"Maybe it's the color you're wearing," suggested the mom.

"Could be the scent of your perfume," the dad chimed in.

Sensible possibilities, but I wasn't wearing any perfume, and my white work uniform was no different than the white shirts of others present.

"Um, I think I'll go visit the monkeys now," I murmured, backtracking as enraged feline snarls filled the air. My trembling finally dissipated as I watched the otters playfully cavorting in their pool, but I just couldn't let the bizarre episode with the lion go. Had she really singled me out? One last look would verify that I had an overactive imagination.

I headed to the cage where both females appeared to be sleeping. Glimpsing me through one slitted eyelid, my nemesis sprang into the same position I'd seen my calico at home assume just before attacking a bug on the sidewalk. The great beast resumed her guttural growling and agitated pacing before abruptly halting directly in front of me with muscles taut and ears at attention. The tension she radiated made my skin crawl. I knew then how a cornered antelope on the Serengeti Plain must feel.

We were in a standoff, this queen of the jungle and I, locked in our respective positions with only a few metal poles between us. Suddenly, I felt an all-consuming itch, the kind that will not be ignored. As I contorted to reach the uncontrollable itch between my shoulder blades, the huge feline emitted a spine-tingling yowl. In a calculated move, she turned her backside toward me and glaring over her shoulder, sprayed me with all the intensity of a fire hose. I was covered from head to toe, my clothes plastered to my body and hair dripping down over my face.

Standing there in shock, I looked down at my ruined wardrobe. I was due back at work within minutes and had no dry clothes. How would I ever explain? Who would believe me? The absurdity of the situation sank in as I watched puddles form around my saturated shoes.

Involuntary spasms of laughter began deep inside me and bubbled to the surface like molten lava. It had been so long since I'd laughed, the release felt strange, foreign. I found wonderful comfort in the realization that God, who knows me better than I know myself, arranged this perfectly ridiculous circumstance to reach down inside the stone that was my heart and begin chiseling from the inside out.

He was chipping away the cold hardness in my spirit and initiating renewal by transplanting a warm, *feeling* heart of flesh. The opaque veil that had engulfed me for so long began to slowly lift and return color to my world.

I can't say that my depression was instantly cured that day, nor would I recommend the lion-spray technique for everyone. But I do know that for me, it was a big (wet) step in the right direction.[1]

> *Lord, You alone are the lifter of my head*
> *[see Psalm 3:3]. Thank You for caring enough to drop a*
> *rope of hope into my deepest, darkest pits. Help me cling*
> *to that rope and climb with all my might.*

Faith in Action

1. Have you ever struggled with depression? (Don't be shy—most moms have.)

2. In Ezekiel 36:26, God promises to remove our heart of stone and replace it with a soft, *feeling* heart of flesh. In what ways has God begun this work in you?

3. How does God's promise to give you a new heart and new spirit plant hope within you? In what ways can you open yourself up to hasten this process?

Note

1. Adapted from "Released: My Experience with the Lion, the Itch, and the (Ruined) Wardrobe" by Debora M. Coty, first appearing in *The Lookout*, October 15, 2006 issue. Used by permission.

13

Grace for Guppies

Childrearing

Call them rules or call them limits . . .
they are an expression of loving concern.
MR. ROGERS

Discipline your children, and they will give you
happiness and peace of mind.
PROVERBS 29:17, *NLT*

A veterinarian friend, Dr. Kathleen, tells about a sick black Labrador Retriever that was brought to her clinic one December. The dog exhibited symptoms of intestinal blockage from something she'd ingested, but the owner was adamant.

"It can't be that. She *never* eats anything she shouldn't!" She paused and added smugly, "I've taught her too well."

Dr. Kathleen hung the poor, ailing pooch's X-rays up to study the contents of her innards. Something looked peculiar. Dr. Kathleen called her assistant over.

"Does that look like a . . . a camel to you?" she asked incredulously.

"Matter of fact, it does," replied the astute assistant. "And there's an angel, a shepherd and baby Jesus, too."

At that moment, the phone rang. It was the dog's owner.

"I just got home and noticed my bare coffee table. Yesterday there was a manger scene there!"

As a young mother, I remember making the naïve decla-
ration, "My child will *never* do that!" Of course, that statement, directly tethered to my ego, implied that I will teach
him so thoroughly (using my superb mothering skills) that
he will rise above the behavior of the common heathen child.

But according to my Theory of Negative Relative-osity
(hey, I can be as scientific as the next guy!), the moment you
state, "My child will never . . ." cosmic forces kick in to ensure that your little darlin' will perform that precise behavior for the rest of his life. Or at least until you attempt to
end his life.

It's no wonder mother guppies devour their young.

Maybe you're blessed with such delightful, well-mannered
offspring that you can actually hold up your head in public.
Or maybe you're like my neighbor Luci, whose son, Marshall,
was the terror of our neighborhood. He routinely destroyed
toys at every house on the block, executed extremely poor
aim when using neighbors' toilets and broke car windows
with his slingshot.

Luci was at her wits' end. She loved her son, but he was
out of control.

One morning over coffee, Luci asked if all the elderly
folks at the nursing home where I worked were cranky.

"Not at all," I replied. "If they were nice when they were
young, most grow nicer as they age. If they were nasty young
people, they become detestable old people."

Her unforgettable response: "Then I sure hope I'm dead
when Marshall turns 70!"

According to Proverbs, discipline is directly related to our
peace of mind as mothers. The problem is in finding what
type of discipline works for which child: a stern look or a blazing paddle? A behavior chart or grounding until graduation?

Even children within the same family react differently to identical methods of discipline. My son responded well to timeout in his room, while my daughter repeatedly slammed her head against the door. I sobbed my guts out that I was the worst mother in the world as she indented the wood with her thick little skull, shrieked and flung her dolls at the wall. (Take heart if you have one of these; she grew into a reasonably-tempered, lovely young lady.)

Don't misunderstand—I'm not advocating one type of discipline over another. I'm just saying that *some* effective form is necessary for that peace we so crave.

The key to seeing discipline through to its positive end result is patience—something most mothers find in short supply because we've used it all up searching for the sock mates that are somehow transported as anti-matter to the parallel universe where alien children hop around on one foot like a pogo stick. Or gathering clothes from the floor to wash, sort and fold, only to find them again sprawled on the floor the very next hour. And discovering on the drive to school that Junior is responsible for two-dozen cupcakes for the party *today*.

I have one word for you, girl: guppies.

"Patience" should be a verb. It's something we do. We may not always *feel* patient, but we must *act* with patience. Surprisingly, the more patiently we respond to our children, the more patient we'll feel.

Fake it if you have to. Pretend you're Noah's wife and you've just been sequestered on an ark with a gazillion animals and a shovel. Or imagine you're one of Solomon's thousand wives and you need a moment alone with your husband.

If all else fails, remember the countless times God has been patient with you and emulate your Father so that your children will one day emulate Him too.

*Shadow of a great rock in a weary land
[see Isaiah 32:2], when my forbearance is shot and
the guppy technique of child management looks
awfully appealing, remind me that patience is
Your thumbprint on my life.*

Faith in Action

1. Read Proverbs 29:17. Now read it again. Try singing it this time. How about a perky rap rendition? Now that it's imbedded in your brain, what does it mean to you?

2. What is your biggest hindrance to providing discipline in your home?

3. Brainstorm three ways you can eek out more patience with your children. (Do it now, *before* the guppy technique is shrieking your name!)

14

Clay-Colored Roots
Heritage

*The family you came from isn't as important as the
family you're going to have.*
RING LARDNER

*Make a careful exploration of who you are and the work you have been
given, and then sink yourself into that. Don't be impressed with yourself.
Don't compare yourself with others. Each of you must take responsibility
for doing the creative best you can with your own life.*
GALATIANS 6:4-5, *THE MESSAGE*

Making a careful exploration of who I am leads me to my
clay-colored roots. During my growin' up years, my family
often trekked to rural north Georgia, my mama's old stomping grounds. Her people had lived in those parts for generations and were the saltlick of the earth (they weren't fancy
enough for a shaker).

Like most families of the Deep South, we were partial to
nicknames. The alphabet was easy enough to wrap your
tongue around, and most of us knew it by heart, so within
our ranks were BB, CC, DD, EE, GG, CL, LaLa and Doll-
baby (who looked more like a prune-baby than a doll-baby).
And, of course, no family on the genteel side of the Mason-
Dixon Line is complete without at least one Bubba—usually
three or four—including the goat, 'coon dog and mule.

Once we'd arrived in the land of cotton, peaches and boiled peanuts (pronounced *bald p-nuts*), I loved to visit my great-aunt EE's country store. She sold bread, flour, slabs of bacon and yard eggs; but the thing I remember most was the glorious low shelf laden with penny candy. She stocked all my favorites—Mary Janes, Pixie Stix, Sugar Babies and Moon Pies. Of course if you had a Moon Pie, you had to have an RC Cola, too (pronounced *aura-cee* in that neck of the words). It was tradition—like cookies and milk, biscuits and red-eye gravy—RC and a Moon Pie. Mmmm!

The store was actually a derelict wooden room nailed onto a shanty that quartered Aunt EE (that's *Ain't EE*), Granny Poss (my great-grandmother), Hawk (EE's crusty WWI-veteran husband) and Hound Dog. Ol' Hound Dog had a bone to pick with children, and whenever one of us inadvertently came near him, he'd bare his pointy teeth and "GRRRR" until we backed off. I always had the feeling that Hawk would've done the same thing in the absence of our parents.

Granny Poss, the family matriarch, was a thin, spidery lady with wild white hair. She occupied a big feather bed in the corner of the *settin'* room. Her voice grated like fingernails on a chalkboard as she screeched out orders to her obliging clan. She sank so far down into the goose-down mattress that her long, bony arm was often the only thing visible above the white cotton sheets. Granny reminded me of the Loch Ness Monster in our *Encyclopedia Britannica*—the slender neck and tiny head a misleading indicator of the powerful entity beneath the surface.

After the county issued a string of health citations about the outhouse (used long after indoor plumbing became commonplace), a tiny bathroom had been tacked onto the house, which sat atop a small hill. Either the foundation had shifted over the years or Hawk wasn't much of a carpenter, for a trip to the privy was an adventure in itself.

You could actually see the grass growing through the gaps in the timber, and the entire room listed to the starboard. The doorjamb was so ill-fitted that you couldn't close the door. The john was so high that climbing on was like mounting a horse. It leaned forward at a 40-degree angle because of the tilting floor, so once you were finally seated, you had to brace yourself with a hand on the wall in front of you or gravity would dump you unceremoniously to the floor. And with the vast array of lizards and bugs that wandered unimpeded through the floorboards, believe me, that was the *last* place you wanted to be.

Looking back, I now see that God used all the circumstances and people—good, bad and bizarre—in my early life to shape me into the person I am today. The person He planned for me to be all along.

And He's done the same with you.

Perhaps your past is not impressive. You may have dealt with poverty, abuse, lovelessness or something equally devastating. Maybe it hurts to compare yourself with others. But God says we don't have to.

We must only take responsibility for doing the best—the creative best—we can with our own lives. And He's prepared each of us for our own special ministry, whether it's serving in children's church, serving stew to the starving or serving up a compassionate hug to a hurting child of God.

Gracious Father, show me the way to be my creative best for Your glory, using all my gifts, abilities, quirks and foibles to sink myself into the unique work You've prepared for me.

Faith in Action

1. In making a careful exploration of who you are (Galatians 6:4), what in your childhood prepared you for your work of today?

2. Who had the most positive influence on your parenting skills? Will your children name you one day when asked this question?

3. What steps can you take to become your *creative* best for God's glory?

15

Sweet Persimmons

Judging Others

*Light travels faster than sound. This is why some people appear
bright until you hear them speak.*
AUTHOR UNKNOWN

*The LORD does not look at the things man looks at. Man looks at
the outward appearance, but the LORD looks at the heart.*
1 SAMUEL 16:7, *NIV*

Remember the maxim, "You can't judge a book by its
cover"? How about "A puckered peel does not a sweet persimmon make"?

Okay, I'll admit I made up the last one. But the gist is
still the same—the façade doesn't predict what's in the
basement. No one personifies that principle any better
than my great-aunt EE (you were introduced to her in the
previous chapter).

Aunt EE was truly an enigma. She was what everyone
called "a real character," which meant that nobody could
tell which of her multiple characters she'd manifest at any
given moment.

With a face like an aging bulldog and a temperament
to match, she was perpetually in a tussle with the county
over one thing or another. If it wasn't the outhouse, it was

the rusting Studebaker enveloped by weeds or the tin can "spittoons" lined up on the store's unpainted porch rail for the old men who sat there chawin' Prince Albert in a Can and spinning tall tales.

By appearances, Aunt EE was big, scary and rough as a corncob, but if she took to you, her snaggletooth grin would make your insides feel like a marshmallow toasted over a campfire.

She generally seemed to like us kids, but Aunt EE was full of surprises too. Once, my obnoxious cousin Howard wouldn't stop whining when my ornery cousin Larry chucked his PF Flyers in the mud hole. Aunt EE gave Howard a pinch of snuff and told him it was licorice gum, just to shut him up. Put a muzzle on him all right. Nothing but retching could be heard from the back stoop for the next half hour.

We all kept a sharp eye on our gum intake after that.

Aunt EE was so "stove up" with "the rheumatiz," she subsisted in a big rocking chair by the pot-bellied, wood-burning stove that constantly belched out warmth in the center of the store during cold weather. Every customer who ventured inside for a can of soup or a jug of milk was expected to stand by the stove for a spell. With hands outstretched or backside protruded (whichever needed thawing most), they'd catch Aunt EE up on the local gossip before laying their coins on top of the ancient cash register. EE rarely counted their money and ran her little business by the honor system.

More often than not, I'd see her silently gesture to some poor soul who'd come in without enough to pay for their tea bags or can of beans, indicating that payment could be postponed until *later*. Even as a child, I knew that *later* would never come for many of those struggling country folk.

Then EE would rock w-a-y back in her rocking chair and launch herself forward, hoisting her unyielding bones out of the rocker. She'd limp over, grab a couple sticks from the woodpile to feed the stove, and open the dairy case, bringing out the big wooden hoop of "rat" cheese (so named, of course, because of its holes). Expertly swinging a meat cleaver, she'd chop squares of cheese to top saucer-sized shortbread cookies from the tall, glass Lance cookie jar on the counter and offer the first Johnnycake to her valued customer.

Folks always left Aunt EE's store walking a little taller than when they came in because they'd been treated with dignity and respect. On face value, you'd never peg Aunt EE as a compassionate person. But, sure enough, burrowed beneath layers of grit and mulishness was a heart that would melt a slab of oleo.

There've been so many people I've misjudged by appearance alone—the intimidating motorcyclist who spent her last $10 on a birthday cake for a handicapped boy; the cranky neighbor who became a "grandpa" to my children; the dirty homeless man who held open my door with a toothless smile.

I'm thankful that when I'm having sour persimmon days—snapping at sales clerks, fuming at bad drivers, grumbling about someone's "stupid" mistake—God looks beneath my behavior. He looks at my heart. And He never gives up on me.

Seer of hearts, please forgive me for jumping to conclusions about people by their outward appearance. Make me more compassionate and less judgmental. I will try harder, Lord, to reflect Your heart within me.

Faith in Action

1. Cite three times you jumped to conclusions about people by their outward appearance. Were you right or wrong?

2. Describe a time when someone misjudged you by your outward appearance. How did it make you feel?

3. What are you doing to teach your children about pre-judging others?

16

Biting off More than We Can Chew

Setting Priorities

The nicest thing about the future is that it always starts tomorrow.
AUTHOR UNKNOWN

But more than anything else, put God's work first and do what he wants. Then the other things will be yours as well.
MATTHEW 6:33, *CEV*

One breezy spring afternoon, as I was watering my yard, an odd rustling in the shrubbery caught my attention. A large flying insect, the likes of which I had never seen before, was caught in some bushes. It looked like a cross between a moth and a bat—bright yellow, with a wingspan of six inches, and a body the size of a Vienna sausage.

Another movement in the mulch alerted me to a garter snake, no bigger than an eight-inch twig, slithering rapidly toward the entangled bug. The reptile was apparently intent on a gourmet dinner, which was rather optimistic, considering that the yellow flying beastie was five times its size. Not the least bit deterred, the snake coiled to strike.

At that moment, the insect broke free from the bushes and began flying low to the ground with the hungry reptile in hot pursuit. The tiny snake caught up to the moth-bat, and reaching upward with open mouth, latched on to the back of one yellow wing.

To my astonishment, the highly motivated insect continued pursuing his flight to freedom, dragging the snake behind him across the lawn. I could see that the yellow fellow was struggling to bear this additional burden, and the reptile refused to relinquish his trophy. Stalemate!

It was time for higher intervention.

Trotting to catch up with the locked-in-combat duo, I stomped my foot hard on the ground. The snake was so startled by this mini-earthquake that he released his vise grip on the moth-bat, which then catapulted like a rock from a slingshot and escaped into the tree branches. Unlike Eden, the serpent lost this battle.

After a walloping good chuckle, I began to see a parallel between my little nature friends and myself. How many times have I bitten off more than I could chew and was overly optimistic in my estimation of all the tasks I could handle? My inability to say *no* caused my plate to get piled high with responsibilities at church, work and community functions. Constantly hustling and bustling, I was serving everyone else at the expense of my family.

Like the pseudo-catastrophe that had stilled the snake, it took a skiing accident and three subsequent knee surgeries to make me stop and reconsider my life goals. God got my attention the only way I would listen—by parking my carcass in bed.

During my year-long recovery, I reevaluated the way I was expending my finite energies during the ever-shortening time my two adolescent children would need me as a hands-on, cookie-baking, there-to-hug-you-when-you-fail kind of mom. Before I knew it, they would be gone, and it would be too late. I would never get the chance to touch their lives in the same way again.

It was a time of establishing priorities and learning to slow down and focus my efforts on what really mattered—the number-one ministry God had given me—my family.

I like to think the little garter snake learned a valuable lesson that day in the garden—perhaps something really profound like, "Dream of filet mignon, but be grateful for hamburger when you're flying on a wing and a prayer."

> *God of the whole earth [see Isaiah 54:5] and all*
> *creatures great and small, help me to constantly*
> *reassess my commitments and concentrate my limited*
> *energies on Your priorities for me. Thank You for the*
> *way You teach me through Your marvelous beasties.*
> *And I'm sorry I ruined the little snake's lunch.*

Faith in Action

1. List your top three energy priorities in order of their importance. (If you're not sure, analyze how you spend your time—the winners will be your priorities.)

2. When was the last time you paused to reassess your commitments and optional responsibilities?

3. Are you spending the finite time you have with your children in ways that will benefit you both in the future? If not, what can you do differently?

17

Prickly Little Arrowheads
Children

Familiarity breeds contempt—and children.
MARK TWAIN

Children are a blessing and a gift from the LORD. Having a lot of children to take care of you in your old age is like a warrior with a lot of arrows. The more you have, the better off you will be.
PSALM 127:3-5, CEV

I can't deny I love the arrows of my family quiver, no matter how prickly their pointy little arrowheads can be. Sure, my children *can* feel like a blessing and a gift—on a good day when they're off at school—but other times, they are definitely a mixed blessing. Like soaking your weary bones in a tub of tepid water.

Now that my son and daughter are both in college, it's supposed to be easier to be their parent. At least that's what everyone told us through the trials of their growing-up years. "Just wait—it's crazy now, but it gets easier!"

That was my only hope during the tantrum phase; the spit-your-oatmeal-as-far-as-it-will-splat contests; the embarrassing, public displays of innocent (and not-so-innocent) shenanigans. As "good" parents, we foolishly encourage our children to ask questions. "That's how you'll learn," we naively say. And then when they do, it's often with disastrous results. Like the day we were crammed into a hotel elevator and my squashed preschooler piped up, "Mom, why do they let fat people on elevators?"

Or the time we were trying to teach my eight-year-old daughter to listen in church instead of daydreaming and doodling on her bulletin. I had just given her a stern lecture in the car about paying attention on the Sunday a visiting minister waxed eloquent during the offertory. "Dear Lord," he began, with arms extended toward heaven and a rapturous look on his upturned face. "Without You, we are but dust . . ."

He would have continued, but at that moment my very inquisitive daughter (who was listening!) leaned over to me and asked quite audibly in her shrill little girl voice, "Mommy, what is *butt dust*?"

Kids—when they're little, they step on your toes; when they're big, they step on your heart!

Then they finally grow up and go to college and are supposed to be able to live independently and make responsible decisions, right?

So how come for Mother's Day my son sends me a get-well card (I wasn't sick) written in Spanish (of which I know nary a word) and wrecks his car three weeks from the date of purchase? And why does my daughter keep buying barrels of clothes when she can't squeeze another shoelace into her constipated closet?

Yet, when I come home from a hard day at work to a sparkling clean house and my daughter bearing a tray of freshly baked triple chocolate chunk cookies with chocolate sprinkles, just for me, or my son calls three nights in a row to see if I'm over my flu yet, I understand that these marvelous people God sent to share my life are indeed like arrows.

They're my weapons of defense against depression, isolation and boredom. They give me joy and purpose that no one else can. And best of all, they mirror my heavenly Father's unconditional love for me, no matter how many motherly mistakes I make.

Father God, thank You for my children—a blessing and precious gift from You. The fruit of the womb is infinitely more rewarding than a banana.

Faith in Action

1. Detail five ways that your children are a blessing and a gift from the Lord (see Psalm 127:3). (Come on, girl, dig deep!)

2. In what ways are your children weapons of defense, like arrows?

3. How are you ensuring by your relationships today that your children will be hanging around in your old age?

18

I Ain't Dead Yet

Aging

I've reached the age where happy hour is a nap.
AUTHOR UNKNOWN

Even when I am old and gray, do not forsake me, O God.
PSALM 71:18, *NIV*

My fortieth birthday dawned cold and bleak. My morning prayers were rote, work was mundane and not one coworker remembered my birthday. I was embedded in the armpit of gloom as I took a shortcut home through rural pastureland.

I felt *old*.

Suddenly, unexpectedly, I glimpsed a sliver of light, the hope of a better tomorrow. There it was, calling my name from a stranger's front yard: a red Honda four-wheeler bearing a FOR SALE sign. My car turned in the driveway on its own accord. I leapt out and stood gawking at the machine that would save me from the curse of the porch rocker. Despite the fact that I had never been that close to an ATV, much less *ridden* one, I was all a-twitter with excitement as a droopy-mustached fellow sauntered over dangling the key.

"Howdy, ma'am. Guess you'll be a-wantin' to take 'er for a test drive," he drawled, tipping his black cowboy hat.

"Oh yes, of course—that would be what I'm a-wantin' to do," I said, my trigger finger itching to get hold of that key. "Now . . . what do I do first?"

The Marlboro Man's cheek twitched. "Well, first ya' gotta get on it." He stared at my bottom half, which was clad in a wool skirt, black hose and patent pumps.

"No problem!" I replied, hitching up my skirt to throw an elegant leg over the saddle, er, that is, vinyl seat.

Maintaining a poker face, he handed over the key and launched into instructions as if I had a clue. "Idles high and takes corners on a dime. It's five up, one down for reverse, brakes high and low."

"Oooookay. But where do I put this?" I flashed my most winning smile as I held up the key.

His mouth twisted into an "S" shape as his eyes screwed shut and his hand rose to rub his furrowed brow. "You've never driven one of these, have you, ma'am?"

"Not recently," I fudged a little.

After the lone ranger v-e-r-y patiently completed my elementary operating course, I popped the gears from first all the way to fourth and the ATV bucked like a bronco. With a look on his face that reminded me of a cattle rustler heading to the gallows in an old Western movie, my reluctant mentor suggested, "Maybe you best keep to the yard . . ."

The tombstone cowboy retreated to his front porch and hunched over, head in hands, while I unearthed a petunia bed, took off a low tree branch, and cut donuts into his front yard. *Yee haw!* What freedom! What release! I felt a kindred spirit to Jane, the jungle woman who swings on vines through the treetops in a mini-dress, swan dives off sheer cliffs and rides an elephant bareback to rescue her man from evil poachers.

As I wrote out a check for my miracle anti-aging machine, it suddenly occurred to me that I had to somehow get it home. The hulking beast certainly wouldn't squeeze into my backseat. I would have to ask Spouse to rent a U-Haul.

He was relaxing unsuspectingly at home when I phoned from my car. "Hi, honey—I'm sorry I'm late, but I stopped to buy myself a birthday present."

"That's great!" he said with sincere enthusiasm. "What did you get, a new dress? A necklace? Those shoes you've been wanting?"

"Not exactly," I replied with growing trepidation. "Are you sitting down? I bought a cute little . . . um, four-wheeler."

"YOU BOUGHT A WHAT???" resounded over the open fields like a cannon shot. After being married to me for 20 years, nothing should surprise the man.

He was a good sport, considering my midlife crisis atonement cost him a bundle to transport home and then up to his parents' remote Smoky Mountains cabin where he thought I could cause the least damage. "Trigger," as I fondly dubbed my twenty-first-century steed, seems very happy there. I go visit him several times a year and together we spend hours climbing every mountain and fording every stream.

Eyebrows all over them thar' hills rise as a *slightly* fluffy middle-aged woman with *slightly* graying hair streaming out the back of her helmet careens down rocky creek beds and rips around high mountain ledges, an echo of hysterical laughter bouncing off canyon walls in her wake. My kids roll their eyes. My husband hides his face.

I'll never feel old again. The Marlboro Man would be proud.

Thank You, Father God, for never forsaking me, especially as I age, and for the fresh joy You trigger in me at unexpected times in my life.

Faith in Action

1. Sometimes we can feel as old at age 26 as we do at 76. What are some things in your life that make you feel old?

2. List three ways God has assured you that He will never forsake you (a good place to start are Scriptures like Deuteronomy 31:8; Joshua 1:5; and Psalm 94:14).

3. What unexpected joy has God brought you during this year of your life?

Raisins Are Merely Patient Grapes

Patience

> *Therefore do not worry about tomorrow. . . .*
> *Each day has enough trouble of its own.*
> MATTHEW 6:34, *NIV*

> *It's smart to be patient, but it's stupid to lose your temper.*
> PROVERBS 14:29, *CEV*

Moms are patient. We have to be or we'd never have kids.

If we didn't have the ability to bend like a sapling in a hurricane, we'd snap. Break. Shatter. We'd forfeit the opportunity to grow, blossom, shield our children with our protective branches, nourish our families with our fruit and provide strength and stability for generations to come.

But patience is not something that comes easily to many women. One would be me. We have to work at it, nurture and develop it over time. Developing patience is like an oyster creating a rare pearl—we shouldn't pray for it unless we're prepared to withstand the grit-grinding process that produces it.

As a children's piano teacher for 20 years, I've learned a lot about adapting to gale force winds and grinding grit. Take that doomed recital for example. But first you have to meet my students.

There's Cat Girl, the musically gifted child who likes to crawl around on my living room floor, rubbing against the furniture and meowing, as she waits for her lesson. I'm not sure if she has an overactive imagination or simply prowls to the beat of a different drummer.

The Calamity Sisters keep me on my toes. The elder steals goodies from my candy dish and stuffs sticky, forbidden wrappers between my couch cushions. Despite threats of maiming by a bust of Brahms, I've often scrubbed smeared chocolate or melted peppermint off upholstery fabric. Once after a lesson, the younger Calamity Sister neglected to tie her shoes and set off down my sloped driveway on her bicycle. When her shoelace wrapped around the pedal, the bike jerked to a sudden stop, bucking her into my brick mailbox stand. There's nothing that builds character quite like supporting a screaming child's broken bones while trying to explain to a hysterical mom how her child broke her hand at a *piano* lesson.

Beautiful Child, the epitome of perfection, is a beauty pageant veteran whose long blonde hair and faultless complexion complement her perfect smile and designer clothes. Mom feels that musical training will round out her myriad accomplishments, which include head cheerleader, a national softball championship and valedictorian of her class.

Fro Bro' is a wiggly little fella who, after dashing through the rain to my front door, shakes his poodle-hair fro like a newly bathed dog, amply watering the roses on my foyer wallpaper. Enduring piano lessons only because his mom makes him, he never knows what songs he's supposed to have practiced or even where his music books are. He prefers to repeatedly kick my piano with the toe of his sneakers while exploring the depths of his nasal passages with stubby fingers about to make contact with my ivory keys.

Conversely, Fair-haired Boy is always prepared and eager to begin. He's a frail, pasty adolescent whose mother tried music in desperation after he tanked miserably in every sport on the planet. Piano turned out to be his forte. He devours musical notes like candy, progressing within two years to advanced training.

Valley Girl is just too, like, busy with her cool friends and after-school activities to hey, like praaac-tice, or, like, answer her cell phone when Mrs. C calls to ask why she's, like, 15 minutes late. Naturally, she's always garbed in the newest fashion rage. I try not to gawk at the shoelace-thin thong peeking inches above her low-rider designer jeans as she sits on my piano bench.

Then there's Inspiring Child, the quiet nine-year-old I rebuked for three months for not concentrating, before her mother revealed that she can no longer see the written music because of a degenerative eye disease. Despite her waning vision, Inspiring Child chose to pursue lessons, painstakingly learning every note and chord by a combination of my verbal repetition and her phenomenal memory.

On the evening of the annual recital, I arrived at the rented church sanctuary to find the doors locked. Not-so-patiently dialing the pastor who'd promised to be there, I got his recorder. GRRRRR. The students and their families began arriving. A half-hour later, the pastor must have finally checked his messages, for the church custodian roared in to open the doors and crank up the AC in the sweltering building.

Fair-haired Boy showed up in a hand splint from flaming tendonitis caused by too much practicing. He was out, doctor's orders. The other students had no time to run through their pieces to iron out the kinks, so we jumped right into the performance.

First up was a duet by Valley Girl and her teenaged cellist friend, who had rehearsed Pachelbel's *Canon in D* beautifully at my house only two days before. Unwisely, I'd neglected to discuss proper stage attire, and the cellist showed up in a miniskirt. Picture, if your heart is strong, a long-legged 16-year-old in a miniskirt, preparing to spread her lower extremities to insert what looks like an enormous violin on steroids between her knees in front of an audience of suddenly attentive adolescent boys and a gaggle of gape-mouthed parents.

I bolted onstage and parked my wide load between the cellist and the audience while my brain whirled with possible solutions. In as calm a voice as I could muster, I suggested that the cellist move *behind* the piano, where she could better communicate with Valley Girl. A collective exhale resounded throughout the auditorium.

After three false starts and Valley Girl's adlib announcement to the audience, "Wow, like—we are *so* messing up!" the girls butchered the beautiful classic and finally retired from the, like, stage.

Cat Girl was next, gliding gracefully through Tchaikovsky's *Concerto No. 1* and purring her thanks into the microphone amidst applause.

While Fro Bro' was skinning his own cat (Beethoven's *Sonata Pathetique* was certainly pathetic that day), I noticed Inspiring Child silently weeping in her chair. Alarmed, I tiptoed behind her and knelt down to ask what was wrong.

"I'm sorry, Mrs. Coty," she whispered, a tear trickling down her cheek. "I can't read the program you gave me. I don't know when I'm supposed to play."

Have you ever had one of those moments when you wish someone would just knock some sense into you with a sledgehammer? In the chaos of our late start, I had forgotten about her special needs. I felt like crying right along with her. "I'm *so* sorry, sweetie. You're sixth and fourteenth," I told her with a hug.

Through the course of the evening, the elder Calamity Sister ripped through an unrecognizable "Fur Elise" at 300 mph, the younger knocked over a potted plant adorning the stage and then dropped the microphone, piercing all eardrums within a five-mile radius. Beautiful Child fled the room in hysterical tears after her second mistake, followed by her ashen-faced mother.

"Only two boo-boos?" I wanted to shout after the young perfectionist. "Big hairy deal! That'd take the grand prize tonight!" But I didn't yell. I didn't cry (yet). I breathed a hotline prayer for patience and dismissed the crowd for warm punch and wilted hors d'oeuvres. And I thanked the good Lord that my oyster would be grinding no more grit for that day!

Great Impatience Doctor, help me remember that patience is the raisin of the fruit of the Spirit. It may grow wrinkled with age but it becomes sweeter as it ripens.

Faith in Action

1. They say patience is a virtue; so how virtuous are you?

2. Name three of the most common matches that tend to light your fuse and threaten to launch your internal fireworks.

3. Okay, now calm down. Breathe. Regroup. What are three practical, *possible* ways you can develop more patience before the fuse flares into a blazing inferno?

20

Rutabagas in Our Tomato Patch

Accepting Others

> *I never judge people . . . unless I have to.*
> SUE BUCHANAN

> *Do not judge, or you too will be judged. For in the same*
> *way you judge others, you will be judged, and with the*
> *measure you use, it will be measured to you.*
> MATTHEW 7:1-2, *NIV*

I realized something was amiss when my daughter's teenage boyfriend commented, "Sweet! A tie-dyed dog!" Sure enough, my dog's ebony hair was electrified with orange, red and yellow streaks.

It all started when he wouldn't stop chewing a hole in his back, just north of his tail. I tried to think of a nontoxic medication that would simultaneously heal and taste so terrible he'd leave the crater alone. Hydrogen peroxide seemed the logical solution, so I'd faithfully applied the stuff to his black, furry backside for five days.

Oops. He evolved into Boy George on a bad hair day.

It occurred to me, as I fed, petted and otherwise lavished love on my pooch, just as I had before his hairdo malfunction, that God takes care of us in much the same way.

He loves us, His children, unconditionally, no matter how our souls are packaged. And we can sure alter the wrappings on our packages, can't we?

One look around my church (especially at the friends of my teens) reveals an immense diversity of earth suits. Few of us resemble the fair little bundles of joy God sent our parents upon our births. We've somehow managed to pierce, tattoo, spike, enhance, tint or inflate these temples of the Holy Spirit that God entrusted to us (see Rom. 12:1).

Yet our heavenly Father looks past our crusty outside trappings to our soft, sensitive underbellies, where we were created in His image. John 3:16 tells us that God loves us so much that *whoever* believes in the gospel of Jesus Christ can hang out with Him for all eternity. That sounds pretty nondiscriminatory to me.

According to Psalm 145:20, "The LORD watches over *all* who love him" (*NIV*, emphasis mine). I'd venture to say that includes believers with pierced tongues, purple hair, gothic attire, eyeball to toenail tattoos or even—heaven forbid—bad breath. But it's not just outward appearance that we must learn to view from God's perspective.

Over the years, I've been involved in a variety of Christian communities, from the extremes of the frozen chosen to flocks of the wild and wacky woolen. Worship styles differ broadly among believers, making it easy to criticize those who (in our humble but accurate opinions) "Amen" too loudly or too often, drop to their knees or raise their hands, sing the wrong kind of songs, dress too casually or worst of all, read from the wrong Bible translation. (Shudder.)

It's so hard to accept rutabagas in our tomato patch.

In a perfect world, all believers would worship their Creator together, unified in bringing glory to God through the diversity of His creation, accepting their differences as God-ordained hues of the rainbow of humanity. In our fallen world, however, where diversity often breeds prejudice, where Democrats detest Republicans, where Christian views are not tolerated (although everyone else's are) and the races struggle to get along, it's miraculous and wonderful that God loves and accepts us just as we are.

Just like tie-dyed doggies.

Master Creator of the universe and all the diverse people in it, help me not to judge others but to recognize and overcome any prejudices I might secretly harbor. And to appreciate the beauty and diversity of that fine rutabaga nestled amid the tomatoes.

Faith in Action

1. Who is the rutabaga in your tomato patch? (Use discretion if she's sitting beside you!)

2. In light of Matthew 7:1-2, think of new ways you can weed your garden without damaging the rutabagas.

3. Rutabagas actually make very good pies. How can you fertilize your rutabaga to enhance his or her (and your) growth in the Lord?

21

Coincidence Is When God Chooses to Remain Anonymous

Trust

*Parenthood has two stages: When your child asks all the questions,
and when they think they know all the answers.*
OLD PROVERB

*Trust in the LORD with all your heart and lean not on
your own understanding; in all your ways acknowledge him,
and he will make your paths straight.*
PROVERBS 3:5-6, *NIV*

While I was sweeping off my front steps one dewy morning,
my cat Sammy-Q came belly crawling along the sidewalk in
fierce jungle cat mode. With bristled fur and taut muscles,
he studied my broom. Apparently deciding it was not friend,
but foe, he attacked the broom head with fangs bared and
claws blazing. I impatiently swept him aside and continued
my chore. Undaunted, he regrouped and launched an air
raid, pouncing from yonder safe distance.

With verbal reproof and growing annoyance, I bodily
removed him from the premises. Not dissuaded in the least,
he returned again and again to attack the evil stick-monster,
regardless of thwarted efforts.

Then a strange thing happened. In an epiphany moment,
I suddenly saw myself mirrored in Sammy-Q's behavior.

Trying on my own initiative to accomplish tasks that I stubbornly refuse to yield to God, my own best efforts often fall short. Seeing only *my* goals, I can't see God's bigger picture. Frustration is the inevitable result.

I could never explain to Sammy-Q the purpose of the broom, nor could he, in his limited capacity as a cat, ever understand my human reasoning for not allowing his misdirected efforts to succeed. We are simply on different levels.

In the same way, I cannot, in my limited human capacity, ever completely comprehend God's divine blueprint for my life. I may *never* see His bigger picture. Like Sammy-Q, I must learn to trust my benefactor's omnipotent reasons—whether I understand them or not—for allowing me to fail.

Sometimes failure is God's way of saying "wait." I sat cuddling Sammy-Q on my doorstep, remembering how this miracle house came to be our home.

The stolen car rolled upside-down on our lawn was the last straw. Our home had been burglarized the previous month and crime had encompassed our Florida neighborhood as orange groves were torn down and replaced by gas stations, strip malls and heavy traffic. We no longer felt safe. Surely God didn't want us to raise our children in *this*. We posted a HOUSE FOR SALE sign the next day.

Two years later the sign, wreathed in spider webs, still flapped in the breeze.

Why wouldn't the house sell? We'd tried everything humanly possible, but to no avail. I'd sprouted calluses on my prayer knees and could not comprehend why God didn't *do* something! Was my prayer channel on mute?

Furiously pumping out my frustration via bicycle pedals one blistering July afternoon, I pleaded yet again for God to move—so we could. Four miles later, I found myself on an unfamiliar street in a rural neighborhood. As I nosed my bike into a peaceful, treed cul-de-sac, my heart began to race. Was that blue house behind the realty sign actually glowing or was it a mirage in the simmering heat? I couldn't tear my eyes away.

This is the one—your wait is over, a still, small inner voice whispered.

It turned out that the house, perfect for our needs, had been on the market for 18 months, and the owners were so desperate they had recently dropped the price $40,000—just squeaking into our price range. Coincidence? I think not.

Stepping out on faith, we put a contract on the house with a contingency that we sell ours within three months. Three months! We'd already been trying for twenty-four!

Back to the prayer rug dimpled with knee indentions. One month passed, and then two. Not even one browser. Whoa—had I gotten my wires crossed? Was God not checking His messages?

It was beginning to look hopeless.

Then one rainy afternoon, I came across Psalm 37:3-5. I knew right away that it was a personal message just for me. "Trust in the LORD . . . dwell in the land and enjoy safe pasture. Delight yourself in the LORD and he will give you the desires of your heart. Commit your way to the LORD; trust in him and he will do this" (*NIV*).

And He did. On the last week of the last month of our contract, we accepted the only offer we'd received during the entire two years the house had been on the market. If it had sold earlier, we'd never have been able to buy the new house, which only became affordable because God had it on lay-away. He'd had a plan all along. I simply needed to trust Him and lean on His understanding, not mine.

Dr. James Dobson has shared the analogy that faith and trust are like witnessing a tightrope walker preparing to cross Niagara Falls, pushing a wheelbarrow. Faith is believing that the fellow can do it. Trust is climbing in the wheelbarrow.[1]

Sovereign God, thank You for being so trustworthy.
Give me a leg up into Your wheelbarrow every morning.

Faith in Action

1. What "coincidences" has God performed in your life during the last month?

2. According to Proverbs 3:5-6, what is the prerequisite for the Lord directing our path?

3. Using the tightrope walker and wheelbarrow analogy, where are you on the faith-trust continuum? Watching from afar? One toe in the wheelbarrow? All or nothing?

Note

1. Excerpts taken from the article "Critter Lessons" by Debora M. Coty, first appearing in the August 15, 2004 issue of *Live.* Used by permission.

Dancing in King David's Shoes
Expressing Joy

*You gave me a new song, a song of praise to you. Many will see this,
and they will honor and trust you, the LORD God.*
PSALM 40:3, CEV

*Let the people of Zion be glad in their King. Let them praise his name with
dancing and make music to him with tambourine and harp.*
PSALM 149:2-3, NIV

After a lifetime of struggle, I have finally accepted my dark little secret. I'm a boogieholic. I've tried to stop, but I just can't help myself. I'm not alone in my shame. There are others.

You know who you are.

Yes, it's true—God gave me the boogie gene. Some people have it, some don't. Those of us who do cannot squelch the uncontrollable urge within us to physically respond to music, regardless of circumstantial inappropriateness . . . juking with our grocery buggies as oldies play overhead, bopping to the radio blaring from the car beside us at a red light, waltzing like Cinderella to elevator Musak. Containing it is like trying to repress the freckle gene.

Impossible.

I married a man who is definitely *not* a boogieholic. Tapping his finger on the steering wheel is an act of wild abandon for him. I thought I could change Chuck in the early days of our marriage. I begged, pleaded and tried to guilt him into dancing with me, but he tactfully suggested we play tennis instead.

So, for many years, I line-danced while vacuuming, swing-danced while cooking, praise-danced while worshiping, and tap-danced beneath my computer desk. I was content with private manifestations of boogie bliss. It was to be my lot in life.

Then, out of the blue one day, Chuck announced he was taking me dancing for our wedding anniversary. I puzzled over his intentions as he whisked me onto the dance floor, but he seemed very self-assured. I soon realized why. He had apparently given this problem much thought and had devised a clever solution. Having been a long-distance runner in his youth, he resorted to what came naturally.

He jogged in place. If the music sped up, he just jogged faster. It was a magical night. I danced myself into an ecstatic lather, and he ran a marathon.

My daughter, Christy, was also blessed (or cursed) with the boogie gene. She was a wiggling mass of dancing baby from the time she could shake a rattle. I even wrote a song for my "Little Boogie Baby," with lyrics like:

> *Prancin' with an upbeat, on tiny dancin' two feet,*
> *Your little face is smiling so sweet.*
> *Mommy loves to watch ya', and Daddy tries to stop ya',*
> *But while the music's going, you're free!*

There's a special joy and exultation in dancing that is elicited from the gut-level release of unfettered freedom. The Hebrew word for dance, *mahol*, also means "whirl; leap for joy." There is a unique purity and beauty of self-expression through joy-filled dancing in which countless cultures since the dawn of creation have reveled. Spirit-directed dancing can draw us closer to God, whether in humble worship or in jubilation over merciful blessings He has bestowed.

King David certainly thought so when he danced before the Lord with all his might in celebration of the arrival of the Ark of God in Jerusalem (see 2 Samuel 6:14). Miriam, Moses' sister, was sure of it when she led all the women in jubilant music and dancing after God's deliverance from the Egyptians after the parting of the Red Sea (see Exod. 15:20).

And I believe God thinks so, too. After all, the boogie gene was His idea.

Lord Jehovah, my strength and my song [see Isaiah 12:2], thank You for the release Your gift of salvation brings to my spirit, and the freedom of joyful dancing. Help me listen today for Your music in my soul.

Faith in Action

1. Do you have a boogieholic in your life? (If it's you, c'mon out of the closet, girl!)

2. How does Isaiah 12:2 apply to you?

3. In what ways do you express the joy of the Lord in your soul? Is joyful expression something you need to develop? (Not necessarily only creative movement!)

The Sword on My Shoulder

Healing

Don't give up! David picked up five stones, not just one,
when he went to face Goliath!
AUTHOR UNKNOWN

I will not abandon you as orphans—I will come to you.
JOHN 14:18, *NLT*

The fields of tall, yellow sunflowers flashed by the windows of our tour bus as the summer sun highlighted the vivid colors of the Israeli countryside. It was June of 2000, and Chuck and I were touring the Holy Land. Little did we know that in a few short months, the ancient country's internal unrest would erupt in bloodshed and tragedy with the first of many bus suicide bombings.

Entering Jerusalem, we passed row after row of gleaming white limestone buildings as our bus navigated the narrow streets. Our destination was Golgotha, the historical site of Jesus' crucifixion, and the Garden Tomb, believed to be the location of His borrowed grave.

We silently gazed at the stark face of the craggy bluff aptly called "The place of the skull." Jagged hollows gave the appearance of grotesque facial features on this cliff where adulterers and thieves were thrown over the precipice, only to be stoned to death by their peers if they survived the fall. The aura of death permeated this place. It was easy to imagine the Roman site of public execution erected at the crossroads in front of the grimacing stone face. It was as if Satan himself was jeering as the very men Jesus had come to save nailed Him to a wooden cross and left Him to die.

The desolation and abandonment felt by the first Christians in this place two thousand years ago became very real to me.

I had recently experienced my own season of spiritual barrenness after five heart-wrenching miscarriages. It seemed as though God refused to acknowledge my countless prayers. So I pulled away from Him. For two long, dry years, my wounded faith lay dormant in the infertile soil of pain.

God's persistent warming touch gradually thawed the iceberg that was my heart and, in time, the hurt inside abated with healing prayer. But maternal yearning lingered like the faint pink hue in the sky after a sunset.

Then came that incredible moment, only four days before our departure for Israel, when my doctor chuckled as he announced the astounding news of my pregnancy at age 42. With our two children in their teens, this was indeed a surprise—accompanied by dark seeds of doubt. Could I possibly keep up with a baby after all these years? If necessary, would my faith be strong enough to withstand another devastating miscarriage?

Drawing me back to the present, Chuck took my hand as we turned away from the harsh death mask of Calvary to enter the lush beauty of the garden surrounding Jesus' tomb. Variegated foliage and beautiful flowering plants erupted in me a surge of joy in the present and hope for the future. The two Marys must have felt the same way when they trod this same winding path to discover an empty tomb and a risen Savior.

Our tour group approached the two-grave cavern carved from the rocky hillside. Absolute emptiness yawned through the gaping entrance and emphasized Christ's power over death . . . and life. My life.

Chuck fell back from the others to take pictures and motioned for me to enter the tomb without him. As I stepped over the track hewn for the large stone that was rolled across to seal the door, my eyes misted with emotion. Pausing on the threshold of the dusky chamber, I realized that I, too, was poised on the threshold of a journey of uncertainty—midlife pregnancy.

I felt vulnerable, so vulnerable.

Entering the tiny cave, I knelt and laid my hand on the crudely chiseled stone cavity that once held the body of my Savior during His most vulnerable time on earth.

Jesus had been vulnerable, too.

Suddenly, I was infused with a renewed faith in God's sovereignty. Jesus had conquered the forces that threatened Him. He'd risen from the dead! There was no power strong enough to keep Him in the grave! The God that ordained an event of that magnitude could surely be trusted to take care of little me.

Comforting peace enveloped me. It was a deep peace not dependent on the outcome of my pregnancy; a peace that surpasses all human understanding.

A week later, we arrived home and eagerly inspected our newly developed pictures. A most amazing thing met our eyes! At the moment Chuck had snapped a photo of me pausing at the entrance to Jesus' tomb, a shaft of sunlight had somehow broken through the surrounding rock walls.

The beam of white light looked like a blazing sword, reaching from heaven to rest on my shoulder.

I have no doubt that God orchestrated the photograph of the sword to be a tangible reminder that His loving touch will always be on my shoulder . . . whatever the circumstances.

Jehovah-Rophe (God, Our Healer), only You can mend that wound deep inside of me that no one else can touch. Thank You for Your penetrating, healing touch and the peace You offer my tattered spirit.

Faith in Action

1. Recall a time in your life when you felt like a spiritual orphan.

2. How has God proven to you that He is Jehovah-Rophe (Our Healer)?

3. Is there a deep wound inside you now that needs God's penetrating, healing touch? Stop right now and ask Him to begin a restorative work in you and slather your heart with peace like a healing balm. Count on Him to do it!

24

One-Way Conversations
Prayer

Prayer is not just spiritual punctuation; it's every word of our life's story.
DEBORA M. COTY

Call to Me and I will answer you, and I will tell you
great and mighty things, which you do not know.
JEREMIAH 33:3, *NASB*

My husband, teenage daughter, her boyfriend and I were seated at the dinner table. The conversation went something like this:

Dad: Great dinner, honey. How about that Oklahoma State game?

Mom: Thank you. Would you like dessert?

Dad: Man, that Joey Graham is something else.

Daughter: What gooey graham? You mean you want a cracker for dessert?

BF: Couldn't be no better, that Graham.

Daughter: Peanut butter? What? You want peanut butter on a gooey graham cracker?

Mom: No, dear, they're in *The Sports Zone*. It's a man thing. We might as well not be here. They can't hear us.

Dad: And Canseco . . . if we can see what Canseco can see, we'd see he can't seesaw on what he saw. José, can you see?

BF: By the dawn's early light . . . play ball!

Daughter: Mo-therrr, what's wrong with them?

Mom: They're on a sports frequency and their antennas can't pick up anything else. Watch this: Honey, how is your Uncle Frank's arthritis?

Dad: Athletics? Yep, Oakland clinched it 9 to 5.

Daughter: Clinched what? Uncle Frank's knees?

BF: No, the Yankees aren't doing so hot in the preseason. Them Sox skunked 'em in the '04 Series and they've stunk up the place ever since.

Daughter: A skunk sprayed their socks? Why don't they wash them in tomato juice?

Have you ever participated in a one-way conversation? The kind where you felt that no one heard what you were saying and the words that did get through were misinterpreted, or worse, ignored.

Jeremiah, the "reluctant prophet," proclaimed God's message for 40 years to an unseeing, unhearing, unresponsive nation (Judah). Not only did they choose to disregard Jeremiah's admonition to repent and turn back to God, but they also cruelly attacked him to the point that he yearned to turn in his prophet badge and retire.

Who could blame him? I would have sacked that job after one day. But he didn't.

Jeremiah continued prophesying to his tormenters, even after they were taken captive and sent into Babylonian exile. Knowing that their dire straits were a direct result of their pigheaded refusal to listen to his warnings all those years, Jeremiah still sent God's message to offer them hope. "Call upon me and come and pray to me, and I will listen to you" (Jeremiah 29:12, *NIV*).

I will listen to you.

Of all people, Jeremiah knew the importance of being listened to. He was intimately aware that unlike many human encounters, God *always* listens when we call upon His name. Even a routine, "Oh, my God!" in casual conversation is a call to the Almighty, and He is indeed listening. After countless false alarms summoning help—like the boy who cried wolf too many times—how can we expect God's immediate attention when we *really* need it?

God wants to have two-way conversations with us, His children. As Jeremiah learned, listening is the essential element to a successful human relationship; and how much more vital is listening in the most important relationship in our lives—that with our Savior.

> *To Him whom my soul loves [see Song of Songs 3:2]:*
> *Help me to be more aware that when I call the Name*
> *above all names, You are listening. Teach me to listen for*
> *Your still, small voice as You speak especially to me.*

Faith in Action

1. Does it bother you to hear God's name thrown about in casual conversation or oaths? Should it? Read Exodus 20:7. Does God think this is important?

2. The media has desensitized us to the flippant use of God's name. What steps can you take to resensitize yourself and your kids to the holiness of God's name?

3. Study Jeremiah 33:3. What two things does the Lord promise to do if we call out to Him? What are some ways God speaks to us?

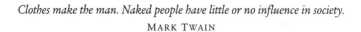

25

"Sag" Is a
Four-Letter Word

Self-Image

Clothes make the man. Naked people have little or no influence in society.
MARK TWAIN

I praise you because I am fearfully and wonderfully made;
your works are wonderful, I know that full well.
PSALM 139:14, *NIV*

Yes, Lord, I do know full well that your works are wonderful, but sometimes I feel *extremely* fearfully made—especially when I see my profile in a mirror!

During a shopping expedition to the local mall, my quest was to locate that most sought-after and rarest of treasures: clothing that camouflages flaws of the 40-something body. Rounding a department store corner, I was confronted by a rack of blouses boldly labeled "Sag Harbor." My eyeballs bulged and my jaw dropped to my not-as-firm-as-they-used-to-be bosoms, which I immediately shielded with crossed arms.

The Bobbing Twins have been hanging there faithfully for more than three decades, and I felt a need to protect Freddie and Flopsie from that offensive "S" word.

Now, I realize that Sag Harbor is an actual place in New York, and I'm sure it's quite lovely in the springtime. But what on earth was the manufacturer thinking when he (I'm assuming masculine thinking processes here) labeled a line of women's clothing a moniker that reminds us *mature* ladies so blatantly of our shortcomings?

"Sag" is a four-letter word in my vocabulary. It's a bad, bad word that discloses in one cruel syllable the havoc gravity is wreaking on my aging body. It's the monster that rears its ugly head when I look in the mirror and see most of the skin on my lower face in a puddle about my chin. It accurately describes the general positioning of my bust, upper arms and buttocks in relation to the trunk of my body.

Yep, "sag" ranks right up there with "cellulite" and "jowls" in my book. Shudder.

I mean, really, if they're going to start explicitly naming women's products after geographical sites, why not launch a line of Buttzville (NJ) panties? A color-coordinated Two Egg (FL) camisole and Superior Bottom (WV) half-slip would complete the lingerie collection.

For that special night on the town, we could shop for a specialty Needmore (AL) push-up bra for complementary cleavage in our new Hooker (CA) evening dress. Naturally, we'd never leave the house without our Hardup (UT) ultra-thick foundation, and mustn't forget our luscious Accident (MD) precision lip liner for that look that demands *Kiss me, you fool!*

If casual apparel is in order, we could shimmy into our Bowlegs (OK) jeans or Big Bonelicks (KN) carefree capris. Add to this a Big Ugly (WV) polka dot T-shirt and open-toed sandals by Toadsuck (AK) for a smashing fashion statement.

Of course, in order to pull off such a brazen display of bodily assets, we'll need to don our Panic (PA) spandex togs and work out regularly on our Spasticville (KS) exercise equipment. This, after indulging in a liquid lunch of Chunky (MI) fat-free, flavor-free faux milkshakes.

So why can't manufacturers emphasize our good points and downplay our liabilities? We women would like to feel beautiful and capitalize on our assets. For us sweetly ripened full-figure gals, how about a line of pretty floral bathing suits (don't you get tired of black, black and more black?) that consolidate and conceal ALL the rear cheek cellulite, labeled whimsically, Humptulips (WA)?

Ooookay, let's get back to the basics of the Psalm 139 scripture . . . praising God for how we are made.

I *do* praise the Lord for the blessing of my fully functioning, healthy body. I am awed by the immensity of my blessing when I lunch with Liz, a 26-year-old stroke survivor who will always limp and never have the use of her right arm again; or when I speak with my neighbor Marcy, who may soon be wheelchair-bound with multiple sclerosis.

I'm overcome with gratitude for my working limbs when I watch my 15-year-old cerebral-palsied niece walk with leg braces and crutches, or when I help amputees like Mr. Byrd don his artificial legs necessitated by the ravages of diabetes.

Come to think of it, I'm thankful that the Twins are there to sag at all, when many women, like my friend Rena, have battled breast cancer and now have prostheses. So when put in proper perspective, my body—and yours—*is* a wondrous and miraculous thing.

I'll try to remember that the next time Freddie and Flopsie drape across my jelly belly as I read in bed.

Strong and Mighty Jehovah [see Psalm 24:8],
You are a gracious provider. I praise You for Your
wonderful works; and today I'm especially aware of and
thankful for the earth suit You have fashioned especially
for me. Regardless of my appearance,
make me altogether lovely . . . like You.

Faith in Action

1. When was the last time you praised the Lord for the creation of your body? (Stop laughing—yes, I said your body!)

2. Name five fearful and wonderful things you are grateful for related to your body.

3. What are two ways you can work on becoming altogether lovely like Jesus (regardless of your appearance)?

Gnawing the Hand that Feeds Us
Gratitude

It's not happiness that makes us grateful;
but gratefulness that makes us happy.
AUTHOR UNKNOWN

I am grieved that I have made Saul king, because he has turned away
from me and has not carried out my instructions.
1 SAMUEL 15:11, *NIV*

God picked Saul to be Israel's first king. He was a choice and handsome man (see 1 Samuel 9:2), a rising star that stood head and shoulders above the crowd. Somewhat timid, too, I would assume from the fact that on his coronation day he hid among the baggage.

What an honor and a privilege for a donkey herder to be crowned king! Can you imagine how Saul must have been blown away by the majesty, power and respect suddenly bestowed on him? It sure beat hopping over donkey dung in the dusty fields! Yet only a short time later, Saul made the conscious decision to repeatedly disobey God, turning his back on the One who gave him everything, grieving God in the process and paving the way to his own demise.

I am reminded of our memorable pet, Freckles the attack bunny. Freckles was a dwarf rabbit no bigger than a powder puff that my daughter, Christy, simply had to have. Things started out well enough with Freckles domiciled in a cage on our back porch. She seemed grateful for her new home and quite agreeable, as far as rodents go.

Not wanting the poor little fluff ball to feel lonely, Christy began chaperoning field trips into the house, which were fine and dandy until it came time to return to the cage. Freckles was intensely resistant to this idea, which resulted in our entire family running all over the house like wild hyenas after illusive prey. Everyone would eventually give up except Chuck, who viewed the chase as a challenging new indoor sport. He'd stalk and corner Freckles, pouncing like a victorious Neanderthal hunter and heroically deposit the squirming animal in its cage.

The sweet little bunny's disposition soon changed.

Freckles forgot who her master was and began viewing Chuck as her mortal enemy. She transferred that animosity toward any human with hairy legs and a deep voice. Whenever unsuspecting post-pubescent males approached, Jekyll-Bunny-Hyde would launch into man-eater mode and attack, sinking her two sharp front teeth into tender ankles, making every attempt to chew her way north. She was nearly un-stoppable—like Bugs on drugs.

What, you may be wondering, did Saul and Freckles have in common? Well, they both began to take their bless-ings for granted and—forsaking gratitude to the provider of their (undeserved) gifts—followed their own selfish courses of action.

Unfortunately, this self-centered attitude is not re-stricted to kings and bunnies. All of us tend to forget our dependency on God when we're blessed with trouble-free periods of life.

When no bill collectors are haunting us, when there's plenty of food on the table, when family relations are harmonious and good health abounds, we become self-sufficient and relegate our relationship with God to the when-I-have-time priority list. We neglect earnest prayer and rely on our own faulty judgment, which we somehow delude ourselves into believing was responsible for the smooth sailing that we now enjoy.

The stories of Saul and Freckles ended in each being dethroned (King David replaced Saul and Freckles was banished to the backyard cage of a progesterone-free household).

In order to praise God, not grieve Him, let's acknowledge daily the One who is truly responsible for our blessings.

Sovereign God, help me always remember that like the air I breathe, I need You all the time, in times of abundance as well as in times of drought.

Faith in Action

1. Have there been any times in your life when you took your blessings for granted? Name them.

2. James 1:17 tells us the source of our blessings. Take a moment right now to thank your heavenly Father specifically for those times of abundance in your life.

3. Cite three examples of people in the Bible who praised God in times of abundance as well as drought.

Just a Humble Blade of Grass in God's Garden

Humility

Lord, make me thoughtful, but not moody; helpful, but not bossy.
EIGHTEENTH-CENTURY NUN'S PRAYER

He is like the light of morning at sunrise on a cloudless morning,
like the brightness after rain that brings the grass from the earth.
2 SAMUEL 23:4, *NIV*

One sweltering summer day, I came home to find the following note from Chuck on the counter. He had waxed eloquent in response to my frequent helpful reminders (some erroneously call it *nagging*) about the sprinklers' inequitable distribution of irrigation, leaving part of the yard deluged and other sections parched.

Dearest Deb,

I fixed the side yard sprinkler and let it run for the full time so all those little plants in the bed ought to feel pretty spunky right now. Most of them were beefing about that one section of grass getting far too much of the water supply—they went on and on about everything being so unfair. So I told them that we would go back to the communism to which they had grown accustomed and give each the same regardless of their needs—even though in reality they don't all deserve or require the same.

I shared with them the parable of the talents (see Matthew 25:14-29) and they all just stood there in stark silence. I could hear faint chatter coming from the rose bed. They were muttering behind their little chlorophyll leaves, "But we're the fairest of the garden; why does that ugly grass get so much water?"

So I went over and plucked one of their fine blossoms and laid it ever so softly in the downtrodden patches of brown grass. There was an audible sigh of gratitude coming from the tiny blades. "We are so grateful for all that we receive, and these exquisite rose petals will certainly spur us on toward greater growth and maturity."

Thus ends the parable of the Coty garden.

Love, Mr. Greenthumb

I must say, Chuck's whimsical little diatribe gave me food for thought about my own place in God's garden of humanity. Am I a self-centered, egotistical rosebud or a humble blade of grass? Do I glory in *my* blooming bouquet of accomplishments (which aren't really mine at all, but simply the results of the Master Gardener's faithful watering and fertilizing), or do I resonate humility and gratitude for the smallest blessings and bits of encouragement?

I fear that my rose by any other name would stink up the place.

My son, Matthew, was a whiz at baseball. It's no small wonder, since Chuck pelted him with balls from the moment he was first able to raise a chubby little arm and bat them away. As Matthew racked up awards and accolades throughout high school, I took them to heart, strutting around the ballpark with my nose in the air, assuming everyone knew *his* accomplishments were *my* accomplishments.

Then, to his doting parents' utter astonishment, Matthew turned down the full college baseball scholarship he was offered, stating that he wanted to be a "regular" kid for a change without the constant performance pressure. Chuck and I crumpled like empty paper bags. We'd somehow forgotten that Matthew's ability came from God and was not our doing. We wanted him to use his talent for our glory—bragging rights—never considering that God might lead him in a different direction.

A few years later, my arrogant rose garden once again burst into bloom.

A competing company heavily recruited me at work. A smug smile lit my face, highlighting the roses in my cheeks. "They must have heard about my wonderful personality and superior work skills to keep pursuing me like this," I gloated. My head swelled to zeppelin size.

Then I overheard a conversation that made me realize it was not *me* they were after, but the account I controlled. It actually had nothing to do with my personal qualifications and everything to do with gaining access to business of which I happened to be gatekeeper.

My zeppelin turned to lead and sank into the deep blue sea.

"Therefore humble yourselves under the mighty hand of God, that He may exalt you at the proper time" (1 Peter 5:6, *NASB*). Ouch. As I read my Bible, it was one of those times when a Scripture seemed to jump out and bite me. By reveling in what I thought were my own accomplishments, I wasn't waiting on God to exalt me; I was exalting myself.

You know, humble pie tastes a lot like liver. Hard to swallow. Nasty aftertaste.

> *Rose of Sharon [see Song of Solomon 2:1],*
> *in Your own way, in Your own time, water me,*
> *fertilize me and prune me into a beautiful (and humble)*
> *rose bush so that I might encourage my own little*
> *rosebuds (children) and the rest of Your garden.*

Faith in Action

1. What does Proverbs 29:23 say about pride versus humility? Do you see yourself as a rosebud or a humble blade of grass? Or something else in heaven's garden?

2. According to 1 Peter 5:6, what does God promise to do if we humble ourselves under His mighty hand?

3. Name a time when you were proud of your humility. (Just kidding!) Of all the people that you know, who would you consider as the best example of a humble person? Name two things you can do *this week* to emulate that person.

A Fowl but Fair Lesson
God Cares

If you bungle raising your children, I don't think
whatever else you do matters.
JACQUELINE KENNEDY ONASSIS

Are not two sparrows sold for a penny? Yet not one of them
will fall to the ground apart from the will of your Father.
And even the very hairs of your head are all numbered.
So don't be afraid; you are worth more than many sparrows.
MATTHEW 10:29-31, *NIV*

It all started with Baby Roadkill, the tiny hairless kitten I plucked off the sizzling highway where she had been abandoned one hot summer afternoon. My mothering instinct kicked in despite my better sense and I blocked traffic to rescue what I thought was a poor mole gone astray.

That started the fur ball rolling. We soon began acquiring canines, felines, fowl and assorted rodents. Enter Mr. Peepers. After our neighbor presented my delighted children with a downy Easter chick, I drew her aside and whispered, "What do we do with it? I don't know anything about chickens, and we have two cats, a dog and a killer bunny . . . that bird's doomed!"

"Oh, those chicks never live very long," she replied, nonplussed. "The kids will play with it a few days and then let nature take its course."

Well, *that* was out of the question after Mr. Peepers began following me around the house like a feathered toddler. The nature folks call it "imprinting," but all I know is we bonded and he became my little biddy buddy.

He didn't die, nooooo . . . he grew into the largest breed of rooster in the Southeast, leering down his beak at the cats that tormented him as a peep. He spent his spare time (when he wasn't following me into the shower or sitting beside me on the couch watching a movie) roosting on a basketball like it was a big orange egg.

Alas, the day came when Mr. Peepers outgrew his sleeping accommodations—two laundry baskets wired together in the garage—and began crowing at dawn as he entered rooster puberty. The friendly neighbor who gave him to us wasn't as friendly when awakened at 5:00 A.M. by *ERR-ER-ERRRRR* reverberating from our garage.

I knew the time had come to cut the apron strings, but I couldn't face my now-enormous chick flying the coop. Reluctantly, I found a farmer who agreed to take him, promising *never* to consider the Kentucky Fried route.

I buckled Mr. Peepers into his seatbelt, and Chuck and I drove him out to the country. The farmer tried to introduce him to other chickens, but shy Mr. Peepers wouldn't budge from behind my legs. After much unsuccessful coaxing, the farmer tactfully suggested we vamoose. Chuck had to persuade me of the wisdom in this, insisting that Mr. Peepers would start acting like a rooster after his human mother was no longer present. As we drove away, I turned and tearfully watched Mr. Peepers chase our car down the dirt driveway.

The farmer said Mr. Peepers eventually adjusted well to his new home and became quite popular with the cute chicks. That's my boy!

I sometimes think of Mr. Peepers when I'm down in the dully-funks. You know—that bottom-of-the-barrel place where your spirits are lower than chicken scratch. If God cares for the least of his fowl creation (I'm betting chickens are even lower in the pecking order than sparrows), then I can take great comfort from the scriptural assurance that He cares infinitely more about the details of the lives of His children.

What a self-esteem booster! My worth is so great to the very creator of the universe, He is aware (and in control) of all the minutiae that sucks up needless hours spent in worry.

*Master of the intricacies of my life, deepen my
comprehension that no beak, feather, speck, jot,
tittle or even hair on my head is too small or trivial
for Your all-caring eye. Thank You for loving me
enough to care so completely. And teach me not
to fret, but to leave the details up to You.*

Faith in Action

1. Do you spend much time in the dully-funks? Are you a fretter by nature?

2. What does Matthew 10:29-31 say about how much God cares about us?

3. List three practical ways you can defeat the joy-sucking dully-funks based on the knowledge that *everything* about you, every detail, is under God's all-caring eye?

Suck a Lemon, Spit the Seeds
Endurance

We are pressed on every side by troubles, but we are not crushed and bro-ken. We are perplexed, but we don't give up and quit. We are hunted down, but God never abandons us. We get knocked down, but we get up again and keep going.
2 CORINTHIANS 4:8-9, *NLT*

God blesses the people who patiently endure testing. Afterward they will receive the crown of life that God has promised to those who love him.
JAMES 1:12, *NLT*

"If at first you don't succeed . . ." I paused in my occupa-tional therapy duties to let my patient complete the old maxim. She was learning the tedious skill of self-dressing with one hand after a paralyzing stroke. Instead of the ob-vious "try, try again," Evelyn reflected on the daunting task before her and replied, "If at first you don't succeed, suck a lemon, spit the seeds!"

Evelyn's words are especially meaningful to me when I'm facing seemingly impossible situations that require patience, humor and, above all, perseverance. It takes spunk to keep spitting those lemon seeds without succumbing to sourness!

Whatever our foe—unemployment, rejection, divorce, abuse, personal loss, illness, chronic fatigue—we may feel beaten down and don't see how we can possibly persevere for another battle in the long war.

Jesus was our best example of endurance in spite of ridicule, beatings, imprisonment, deception and desertion by his closest friends. People failed Jesus again and again. But He rose above disappointment and hurt and kept His eyes on His deeper purpose—ministering to the very ones who had wounded Him most.

The Bible brims with role models of perseverance.

Ruth, who tragically lost her husband, friends and home, chose to follow God's guidance to accompany her mother-in-law to a foreign country, where Ruth was *different*. Yet if she hadn't persisted through that painful process, she wouldn't have been in position to love again and complete the lineage that produced King David and, later, Jesus Christ. (Read about her heartwarming love story with Boaz in the Old Testament book of Ruth.)

Hannah (see 1 Sam. 1–2) also persevered through long-term suffering; not only did she have to share her husband with another woman, but she was also barren—a public disgrace in her day. For years she endured the taunting of her rival. Hannah was greatly distressed and wept bitterly; but here's the kicker: she kept on praying. The Lord mercifully blessed her with her heart's desire, and Hannah's child grew to become the mighty prophet Samuel.

We don't know all the details of what motivated Hannah and Ruth to keep going when life got tough, but for modern day moms, a vital element is a dynamic support system. This is something that doesn't magically happen without us doing the legwork to seek and find those with whom our hearts connect. Spouses are a good start, but (no offense to the hairy sex) they're not enough.

Girls need girlfriends, not just in their youth but also throughout their life. You and I need soul sisters with whom we can spill it, cry, giggle, act silly and just plain chew the fat (including white chocolate macadamia nut cookies!).

Families are a natural support system, but if blood-family is not an option, we can develop spirit-family who will faithfully hold up our needs in prayer. Such heart-bonds can be found through support groups, Bible studies and prayer partners. These allies in Christ are the first to bring food during illnesses, help with physical tasks and care how you *really* are. Like life preservers in a turbulent sea, prayer partners are buoyancy for the soul and security through storms.

Personal restoration is another essential when we're depleted. Reenergizing is individualized, so try different things to see what works for you—perhaps it's reading an inspiring article or book (like this one!), creative expression through painting, writing, or cooking (unless you cook like I do, which is indeed creative but often inedible).

How about taking a moment to bask in the sun or dig in the garden? For me, a quickie refresher is bopping to some upbeat Christian music or taking Ol' Bess (my bike) for a spin around the neighborhood—just me, my Papa God and His creation.

As long as we're alive and kicking, we'll have to contend with those lemon seeds of endurance. We can either avoid lemons altogether (do nothing so we'll never fail), swallow the seeds (accept defeat and quit) or take another lemony bite out of life and persist in spitting those seeds.

My Strong Rock [see Psalm 31:2],
fill me with hope through the hard times.
Help me pucker up, persevere and keep
on spitting those lemon seeds. Ptooie.

Faith in Action

1. Who would you say is your soul sister? How did you first connect with her?

2. Which is your tendency in dealing with the lemons of life: Avoid all citrus, swallow the seeds, pucker up and take another bite? Why?

3. Name three reenergizing techniques that would work for you. (Examples are given at the end of the chapter, but be creative based on your own circumstances.)

Can't Take Many More Surprises!

New Life in Christ

Life is too important to be taken seriously.
OSCAR WILDE

If anyone is in Christ, he is a new creation;
the old has gone, the new has come!
2 CORINTHIANS 5:17, *NIV*

Not a creature was stirring, not even Debbie the grouse, which is why the muffled BOOM awakened me just before midnight on Christmas Eve. I sat straight up in bed, my sluggish brain a tangle of confused thoughts. *Was that really a noise, or did I dream it? Did Santa land on the roof?*

Jolly-old-elf Chuck, who was assembling Christmas toys in the living room, opened the bedroom door just as a wave of horrific odor rolled across the room and simultaneously slapped us.

"Good heavens, what in the WORLD is that stench?" I choked out, jolted fully awake.

"I don't know," Chuck answered. "I thought I heard something strange in here. I figured either you fell out of bed or a reindeer put a hoof through the ceiling."

"There's something moving in the closet," I whispered, slipping out of my warm, cozy bed to bravely face the mysterious monster that was no doubt crouched to leap out and utterly destroy us. It had to be the creature of the black lagoon to reek like that.

As Chuck and I cautiously crept into the walk-in closet with only the pale glow of a nightlight illuminating the blackness, we struggled to decipher what our unbelieving eyes were seeing. A thick, dark substance like chocolate pudding splattered his hanging shirts and covered my shoes. The offensive goo was dripping off the walls and pooling on the carpet.

"What *is* this stuff? It smells like somebody blew up a truckload of rotten eggs in here," Chuck groaned, looking around in disgust.

"I'm afraid somebody *did* blow up," I replied, staring in horror at the purring ball of feline fur at my feet. Our cat had been acting peculiar for the past week, and amid the hectic Christmas preparations, there had been no time to take her to the vet. Our snowy white cat, now mostly brown and sticky, sported a gaping hole in her side like a newly erupted volcano. She looked up at me with a relieved kitty expression on her face, as if to say, "Ah . . . do I feel better!" I tried to find a clean spot on her head to scratch.

So instead of worshipfully thanking our Creator for the gift of His Son, the wee hours of Christmas morning found us cleaning, disinfecting and comforting His creation. The creature (cat) fully recovered from the internal abscess that created mounting pressure until it burst forth like a cannon firing.

As I scrubbed the closet on all fours, I couldn't help but draw parallels with 2 Corinthians 5:17. When we become new creatures in Christ, we expel the old, festering sin in our life and start over fresh . . . like Kitty, who was practically dancing on tippy-paw in relief and freedom after her physical nastiness was expelled. The *only* way to experience that kind of new spiritual life is through faith in Christ.

So if you haven't yet received the gift of salvation your heavenly Father offers through His Son, consider that you may be walking around with a putrid, infected heart inside of you. The Great Healer can excise that and replace it with a bigger, greater, more joy-filled heart than you've ever known.

Just ask Him.

And you probably won't even have to scrape the blobs of alien pudding off your walls afterward!

Friend of sinners [see Matthew 11:19], thank You for expelling my vile, rancid putrescence and filling me with your freshness and joy, new every morning.

Faith in Action

1. In what ways have you become a new creation in Christ?

2. Ephesians 4:23-24 implores, "Let the Spirit change your way of thinking and make you into a new person" (*CEV*). Name two ways God renews you with freshness and joy. (Examples: the beauty of a sunset, playing with a roly-poly puppy, the purity of a sunbeam bursting through rustling leaves, cuddling your baby on a frosty winter evening . . .)

3. Name three people in your life who need the gift of a joy-filled *new* life in Christ. Stop and pray for them right now. Think of ways to share Christ's love with them.

Burn, Baby, Burn

Encouraging Others

*When they were discouraged, I smiled and that encouraged them,
and lightened their spirits.*
JOB 29:24, *TLB*

Therefore encourage one another and build each other up.
1 THESSALONIANS 5:11, *NIV*

Shortly after I began freelance writing, I was standing in the lobby of my church, speaking with a friend. Bubbling with excitement on the coattails of my third magazine article acceptance in as many months, I'd just begun filling in the glorious details when an acquaintance walked by and abruptly halted to inject her unique perspective.

"Excuse me," Miss Buttinsky said, doing just that. "Did I overhear you say you've begun writing—as in being *published*?"

"Why, yes," I replied, naively expecting congratulations for my accomplishment.

"What exactly qualifies *you* to be a writer?" she asked with a look on her face that brought back memories of my irritated mother asking 10-year-old me if my filthy room was clean yet. Without waiting for my reply, she continued. "Did you major in journalism in college?"

"Um, no." I wondered where she was heading with this.

"Were you an English major?" Her words were crisp and well enunciated.

"Not exactly," I answered sheepishly, beginning to feel as if a heat wave was rolling through the room.

"How, then, are you qualified to be a writer?" she asked, crossing her arms and cocking her head to one side.

Flabbergasted, I glanced at my friend, who was looking back at me with her mouth hanging open. With sudden divine inspiration, I nodded my head and shrugged. "You're right. You're absolutely right. I'm *not* qualified to be a writer. But you know something really funny? There are three editors out there who think I am!"

I'm often saddened that we Christians don't try harder to encourage and build each other up. Blowing out someone else's candle doesn't make ours burn brighter. It only makes the world a darker place.

One of the best—and easiest—ways to encourage others is by sending notes to those who are hurting or discouraged (just look around—we're surrounded by them!). Although phone calls and e-mails are beneficial, I've found that cards are appreciated for their read-and-reread quality and the ease of soaking in the message of encouragement privately without pressure of immediate response.

A note that reminds someone "God loves you!" and "I care!" can become a little oasis of love in the desert of a bad day. This is especially true with our children, who receive their lion's share of encouragement from us, their moms. I developed the habit of slipping little love notes in my children's lunchboxes or doodling hearts or hugs and kisses symbols on the napkins I tucked beside their sandwiches. My daughter often reciprocated, and special cards I've received from her are taped to my mirror to continuously uplift me.

Probably the most effective way to encourage someone is to *listen*. Time can be the most difficult but precious gift of encouragement we can give. In this age of bustling busyness, offering others our physical presence affirms their personal worth. Active listening includes eye contact, thoughtful comments or questions to clarify what was said and follow-up responses motivated by genuine concern.

This is a real challenge for me. With the nanosecond attention span of a tweety bird, I must exert maximum energy to stay focused when a friend is pouring her heart out, or my husband is telling me about his day. My mind flits ahead to the tasks I will tackle as soon as the conversation ends.

Fixating on the speaker's nasal hair or front teeth keeps my attention centered. Gross maybe, but it works for me.

We can tangibly encourage others by meeting their physical needs. I once observed that the hard-working mother of four young sons always wore the same threadbare sweater to church each Sunday. Tight finances kept the growing boys in clothes, but left little extra cash. I anonymously mailed her a small sum earmarked for a sweater, accompanied by a note extolling her excellent example as a Christian mother.

My heart flooded with delight when I saw her the following Sunday, face glowing and shoulders a little straighter beneath a new blue sweater.

For some reason, it's often easier to encourage those outside our home than family members we rub up against every day. Friction has a way of scraping our good intentions raw. But it *is* possible if we focus on flicking the wicks of the little ones we love. After all, when they burn brighter, we glow too!

Our willingness to give of our limited time motivates our children to go the extra mile with those souls God has placed in the course of their day.

Kindness begets kindness. Encouragement spawns en-couragers.[1]

Master Encourager, thank You for esteeming me as Your beloved child. Help me build up someone today—to kindle his or her candle, not blow it out.

Faith in Action

1. Can you recall a time when someone encouraged you at just the right moment?

2. List five ways you regularly encourage others (e.g. listening, writing notes, cooking their favorite foods, attending their events, spending a little TLC time).

3. Brainstorm some ideas for further encouraging your children.

Note

1. Excerpts taken from "Freefall Into Freelancing" by Debora M. Coty, first appearing in the July/August 2005 issue of *Writers' Journal,* and "Just What They Need: Six Ways to Encourage Others" by Debora M. Coty, first appearing in the May/June 2005 issue of *Discipleship Journal.* Used by permission.

Ferrari or Minivan?

Investing in Family

We never know the love of our parents for us until we become parents.
HENRY WARD BEECHER

*What you receive from me is more valuable than even
the finest gold or the purest silver.*
PROVERBS 8:19, *CEV*

My extended family decided to try a new restaurant for a
birthday celebration. The hostess led our large party to a
table, and we began studying our menus.

"Good evening, everyone, are you ready to order?"

A shockwave rocked my solar plexus and all the air
sucked out of my lungs as my eyes locked with those of our
server. My jaw dropped. Her jaw dropped. It couldn't be!
Or could it?

"Megan!" I cried, wide-eyed. "What are you doing here?"

Her face flushed as she suddenly found her shoes very
interesting. "I'm working," she said in a small voice.

Fifteen years earlier, Megan had been a millionaire,
wife of a successful executive in my husband's multilevel
company. Megan lived a lavish lifestyle and used her wealth
to encourage us lower-level wives to motivate our husbands to work harder (her husband received commission
on their production).

She took me on her personal shopping sprees (I watched in awe as she spent thousands of dollars), invited me to help redecorate her house, gave me her hand-me-downs (which were much better than what I had) and insisted that I try on her new full-length mink coat and matching hat.

"You can have all this too," she whispered, a coy smile on her lips, "if you just get Chuck out there devoting 100 percent of his energy to creating new business."

But neither Chuck nor I were willing to pay the price of his constant absence from the lives of our children to attain the wealth she touted. Chuck eventually left that company for one with less income potential but which allowed him flexibility to schedule around the needs of his family. He never missed one ball game, school play or family outing because of work. We decided it was more important to invest in the lives of our kids than in the stock market.

So there was Megan, many years and mega-bucks later, standing before me in her stained waitress uniform, a mere shadow of the socialite she had been. Her shoulders were rounded, her face careworn, her once-styled, raven hair now pony-tailed and gray-streaked. I learned that she had eventually divorced, and lost her beautiful mansion, sports cars, everything. The chic crowd she considered friends disappeared. Her only child had incurred enormous medical bills with a near-fatal illness, and she had to work long hours to make ends meet.

I was speechless. Stunned. I could barely eat the food Megan placed before me. Several times during the evening, I glanced across the room to find her misty eyes on my laughing, boisterous family. Sadness filled me—for Megan and for the multitude of people like her who choose wealth as their life goal.

Psalm 128:1,3 promises, "The LORD will bless you if you respect him and obey his laws . . . just as an olive tree is rich with olives, your home will be rich with healthy children" (*CEV*).

We're not wealthy. Never have been and never will be. Sure, I was sometimes envious of Megan's *stuff* and wouldn't be honest if I didn't admit to dreaming of my own thousand-dollar shopping spree. But *stuff* is only temporary. It'll all burn one day.

I wouldn't want a Ferrari anyway—just something else to keep clean besides the kids, the dog and the kitchen sink, all of which must fit into any vehicle I own.

Give me my trusty, beat-up ol' minivan any day. It's broken in just the way we like it. Plus it smells comfortingly of brownies, corndogs and homemade chicken salad with a smidge of honey mustard.

Well, there's also an underlying aura of dirty sneakers and a lingering musky odor from when the mama raccoon and her three babies ventured into our garage through the cat door and explored the exciting cave on wheels they found there.

Raccoons, of course, prefer to clean their food before eating it, so the little critters dipped pawfuls of dry cat food into the water bucket to create a kind of Friskies paste, which they then tracked all over the van cave. By morning, their footprints had hardened into cement, like fossilized tracks of tiny prehistoric dinosaurs.

You just gotta love a mama who insists her offspring wash up before dinner!

And then one fateful night, the littlest coon dude squeezed through the three-inch window opening and got *inside* the van cave. For the weak of gut, we won't go there.

Back to my point: Money can be lost in the twinkling of a bank vault key. But God's enormous blessing—our families—will warm our hearts forever.

It's our choice how we invest our time and energy.

Bestower of Blessings, help me really appreciate the rich blessing of my family and focus on my wealth of love instead of my love of wealth.

Faith in Action

1. What does Psalm 128:1-3 promise if we respect the Lord and obey His laws?

2. In what ways do you consider your olive tree (home) rich with olives? How do you fertilize your olive tree to ensure healthy olives?

3. Would you say most of your time is currently spent pursuing a wealth of love or a love of wealth? Are you satisfied with this?

Pl-a-a-ay Ball!
Sportsmanship

We don't stop playing because we grow old;
we grow old because we stop playing.
GEORGE BERNARD SHAW

We put no stumbling block in anyone's path,
so that our ministry will not be discredited.
2 CORINTHIANS 6:3, *NIV*

What's a mom to do as she slumps in the bleachers, witnessing her mild-mannered husband's transformation into a hulking monster over an umpire's call while her wide-eyed, thumb-sucking first grader intently watches from the dugout?

How does she explain the soft drink that she *accidentally* sloshed on that obnoxious fan rooting against her son's team?

Having had a child involved in organized sports in soccer, softball, baseball, gymnastics and basketball seasons for more than a decade, I've become something of an enigma in my community.

"Oh, no—put on your raincoat! It's that crazy Coty woman again!"

Hey! Aren't we *supposed* to get out there and support our offspring by involvement in their activities? Doesn't our input demonstrate concern? Certainly that must include expressing our opinions on everything from the near-sightedness of the referees to the insanity of the coach's choice of uniform colors (I insist on gray, which everything else becomes after a few games anyway).

We've all seen them. Most of us have been them—over-zealous parents who scream, spit and spew, caught up in the delirious frenzy of competition. The image of Christ demonstrated by His followers often becomes decidedly blurry at sporting events . . . like a photograph out of focus.

Somehow it's socially acceptable to say and do things at a ballgame that we would never consider doing anywhere else. A well-dressed woman once threatened to "body slam" me if my son beat hers for a position on the All-Star team. On more than one occasion, I've been sorely tempted to stuff my pom-pom down the cleavage of an overly enthusiastic mom. Spouse once narrowly escaped a punch in the jaw from an irate opposing dad. A friend decked a referee with her purse as he ran down the sidelines.

What about the rotten sludge-flinging from the mouths of spectators? Hostility and name-calling produce negative attitudes, which have a cumulative effect on everyone involved, often snowballing into an avalanche of devastation that can bury people—including our children—alive.

We passionately love our kids and want them to succeed. Sometimes that passion becomes misdirected in an "us against the world" mentality, especially in sports, where human error—by referee, coach or player—is often misinterpreted as an intentional assault against our child. This (perceived) injustice enrages us. It inflames our righteous indignation and "fight for what's right" impulses. We overreact, rallied on by the emotionally charged environment.

We get downright *ugly*.

So how do we as Christian parents steer clear of the shouting matches and distasteful behavior we're sometimes drawn into modeling for our children?

Our hardest task is to channel our enthusiasm—and opinions—productively, so that we remain ambassadors for Christ while uplifting our child and his teammates. "Be completely humble and gentle; be patient, bearing with one another in love" (Ephesians 4:2, *NIV*).

A good rule of thumb is to cheer *for* the kids rather than *against* the opponents. For example, "Nice catch, Tommy!" instead of (addressed to the nine-year-old batter) "Ha! You can't hit squat, ya little creep!"

In the sports arena, with our fangs exposed, it's hard to tell the difference between the Christians and the lions.

Preparation is important. I've found that prior to each event, it's imperative to ask myself: *Is my primary purpose to glorify God in this place? If so, how will I achieve that goal when tensions rise and tempers flare?* I can either influence others toward Christ or repel them.

Making a peace plan and sticking to it can diffuse many a potential bomb before it detonates. It's best to discuss this issue with your husband during a quiet, sane time at home (good luck finding one!). Chuck and I use a prearranged system of cues to keep each other in check when approaching that dangerous, out-of-control place: a touch on the arm, humming "This Little Light of Mine" or a strategic trip to the concession stand in order to momentarily remove ourselves from the premises for a renewed perspective. In other words, go chill out on a chocolate bar. Breathe deeply. Regroup.

It's never easy to retreat in the heat of battle. I think the devil is the world's biggest sports fan because that's where

Christians are the most vulnerable to being reduced to nasty, vile creatures when their spiritual armor is down. But we *can* win by bolstering our spiritual armor with the shoulder pads of righteousness, the catcher's mitt of faith, the batter's helmet of salvation, the cleats of the gospel and the bat of the Spirit.

Once we've suited up, let the games begin!

Mighty God, thank You for coaching me in this game of life. Help me get off the bench, firmly insert my mouth-guards of discretion, and score points for eternity.

Faith in Action

1. Does someone in your family morph from meek Dr. Jeckyll to tyrannical Mr. Hyde during sports events?

2. Think about your child's competitive events for the last month. Name two potential stumbling blocks in your public behavior that might discredit your ministry for Christ (don't be embarrassed; we all have them!).

3. Study Ephesians 4:2. What are some techniques you can implement to become more "patient, bearing with one another in love" (*NIV*)?

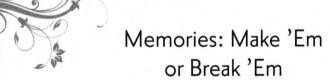

Memories: Make 'Em or Break 'Em

Creating Positive Memories

It is the sweet, simple things of life which are the real ones after all.
LAURA INGALLS WILDER

Only be careful, and watch yourselves closely so that you do not forget the things your eyes have seen or let them slip from your heart as long as you live. Teach them to your children and to their children after them.
DEUTERONOMY 4:9, *NIV*

Your son kicks the game-winning goal; your little gymnast scores a 9.4 on the vault; your 10-year-old hits his first home run. Such are the makings of wonderful family celebrations that turn into lifelong memories.

But what happens when your daughter fumbles the flyer at the cheerleading competition or your son strikes out with bases loaded? Unfortunately, such disappointing moments are also part of the nature of sports, the stuff of not-so-nice memories. Dreaded as they are, they *will* happen, and how we as parents deal with them can make or break the spirit of our children.

Experiencing the agony of defeat is an opportunity to teach our children the spiritual lesson of perseverance in fighting the good fight and finishing the race, as Paul so aptly describes in 2 Timothy 4:7. He didn't say anything about winning or losing; the important part is *finishing*. God doesn't love us any less if we come in first or thirty-first.

For the purpose of increasing endurance, my tennis coach insisted I join the cross-country team in eleventh grade. I routinely came in seventh out of eight runners. Only one poor slug was slower than me (but she got so sick of last place, she ran all summer, and the following fall she won district!). I didn't relish losing, but I never stayed discouraged long because I knew when I crossed that finish line God loved me as dearly as if I'd won Olympic gold.

Demonstrating unconditional love to our children after poor performances mirrors the unchanging love of our heavenly Father for us, despite our mistakes and shortcomings. With the prevalent worldview urging "discard the useless," we may be the only source of positive reinforcement our children have when they fail.

When my daughter's disastrous turnover during the crucial final minute of a high school basketball game made her the proverbial goat instead of the hero, I tried desperately to think of something to lift her discouraged spirit. Unable to come up with anything profound, I propped a handmade poster on her bed proclaiming, "You played your heart out! We are PROUD of you!"

She arrived home after the game and went straight to her room with her head down and shoulders slumped. I peeked around the doorframe to see her clutching that crude sign to her chest, silent tears dripping down her face. She cherished that simple symbol of her value to her family and displayed it prominently on her wall for years.

Parental encouragement after a loss teaches a child that her worth in God's eyes (and her parents') is not dependent on her skills or production; and just because she may lose, she's not a *loser*. A Christlike attitude and demonstrating God's grace under fire determines who is a *winner*, not the score of a game.

What will our children remember about these years? Our parental role is pivotal in forming future positive memories and influencing what kind of parents our children will be.

Ross, an excellent baseball catcher with college prospects, quit the team in his senior year because of his dad's incessant criticism of his performance after every game. Jason was an award-winning shortstop whose father refused to speak to him for days after "bad" games. Both boys are now men and have bitter memories of what should have been some of the best times of their life.

One of my most significant sports memories was when I was 16, playing a high school tennis match. I was so rattled the first time my mother showed up to watch (the last match of the season) that I lost my concentration and totally fell apart. She finally left so I could focus on my game. That night, my mom apologized for not having been more supportive. After that, she made an extra effort to come out and cheer me on. To this day, I consider Mama my biggest fan.

Do our children consider us their biggest fans or their worst critics?

Heavenly Father, help me to be mindful that
I'm creating memories, good or bad, every moment
of every day with my children. Give me the wisdom
and energy to do whatever it takes to ensure that
I'm president of my child's fan club.

Faith in Action

1. What is one special memory from your childhood (related to your parents or guardians) that you hold dear? (Doesn't have to be related to sports.)

2. What made that memory so significant to you?

3. How are you currently making your child feel like a *winner* in your eyes (and thereby creating precious memories)?

Harried Porter
Self-Control

Those who live by the sword get shot by those who don't.
AUTHOR UNKNOWN

Don't use foul or abusive language. Let everything you say be good and help-
ful, so that your words will be an encouragement to those who hear them.
EPHESIANS 4:29, *NLT*

Manners. Have they really gone the way of dinosaurs? Drivers on any crowded highway in urban America will agree
they're rarer than Brontosaurus toenails.

Those of us raised in the Deep South have no excuse for
poor manners. "Yes, ma'am" and "No, sir" were drilled into
us at the risk of meeting Mama's switch behind the shed.
None of this addressing elders by their first names; adults
were called "Miz" or "Mister" by everyone younger, even by
as slim a margin as one year. A close friend of the family
might be honored with the title "Miss Annabelle" instead of
"Miz Jones," but that was a privilege earned by respect.

For Southern women, apologizing used to be considered a necessary tool to getting along with others. Apologize
first; clarify later. I think this was supposed to cast us in a
meek, ladylike light, regardless of the biting steel of the
magnolia beneath the veneer.

Even now, I find myself apologizing for the most ludi-
crous things; when sneezing in my car, I ask my steering

wheel to please excuse me. I beg for pardon when bumping an empty chair. I even apologized for my behavior in my daughter's dream (she dreamt I was dawdling to wash my hair while a crazed killer was breaking into the house).

Unfortunately, this mannerly attitude toward inanimate objects doesn't always spill over to flesh-and-blood humans on highways or at checkout counters. I'll never forget the horrifying reality check when my five-year-old asked, "Mommy, why do you talk to the cash register ladies so mean?"

Mean? I thought I was being *firm* and *assertive* (both socially acceptable terms). But truthfully, on the Jesus spectrum of human relations, I was bordering on abusiveness by my demanding and unforgiving "I'm-the-customer-and-therefore-always-right" attitude.

Road rage has become an expected (albeit still frowned upon) part of the American driving experience. I find it frightening to witness the dark side of those I love—especially myself—bursting forth when hunched behind a wheel, spewing venom, muttering threats, wishing evil on other drivers. What would Jesus think of us if He were physically seated beside us in the passenger seat?

My driving behavior nosedived to such an embarrassing low that I scraped the "Jesus is my Co-pilot" bumper sticker off my car to conceal my identity as a Christian. Instead of handing over the controls and making Jesus my pilot, I ejected Him from the cockpit altogether.

When my daughter obtained her learner's permit, I was shocked to see her morph into mini-me within days of her first driving experience. It was like watching sweet little Princess Leia climb into the cockpit of the Death Star and begin channeling Darth Vader.

"What an idiot!"

"Look out, you big jerk!"

"Somebody needs to teach that airhead how to drive!"

I realized with shame that my daughter was only regurgitating behavior she'd witnessed during the first 15 years of her life.

After all, there's no hotter racetrack on earth than the morning school drop-off line. All those harried porters jockeying for position, determined to deliver their backpacked, runny-nosed cargo and make it to work/exercise class/Bible study on time.

You snooze, you lose, sister. The courtesy you learned as a child is now a handicap, a weakness. If you so much as reach down for a tissue, the teeth-gritted, maniac mama in the Hummer beside you edges you out when the line moves a quarter inch. Glares scorch, horns blare, fists pump and nostrils flare routinely among ordinarily friendly women who would on any other occasion sit down together for laughs and lattes.

Do I *really* do that much name-calling behind the wheel? The sad truth is, I do, and my children are there in the backseat, like dry sponges in a mud puddle, taking it all in.

What does the Bible have to say about that?

"You're familiar with the command to the ancients, 'Do not murder.' I'm telling you that anyone who is so much as angry with a brother or sister is guilty of murder. Carelessly call a brother 'idiot!' and you just might find yourself hauled into court. Thoughtlessly yell 'stupid!' at a sister and you are on the brink of hellfire. The simple moral fact is that *words kill*" (Matthew 5:21-22, *THE MESSAGE*, emphasis added). Whoa. Strong words. Strong judgments.

So, Lord, what's a crazed mother to do?

"Your attitude should be the same as that of Christ Jesus: Who, being in very nature God, did not consider equality

with God something to be grasped, but made himself nothing, taking the very nature of a servant, being made in human likeness" (Philippians 2:5-7, *NIV*).

Okay, let me get this straight, Father. You want me to
empty myself like Jesus did, deliberately taking on the nature of a servant?

Indeed—the nature of a servant.

But Lord, servants actually *serve* people! You're asking
me to really *see* those people out there—the clerks and wait-
ers, phone solicitors and crazed drivers—as beloved children
of God, just like me?

*Yes, my Debbie. They're preoccupied people simply trying to do
their jobs and fulfill their responsibilities—just like you.*

But God, I can't pull that off.

*Probably not with your own strength. But that's what I'm
here for.*

*Master of the tempest, help me master my
temper and remember to converse with you instead of
jockeying for position in the fast lane.*

Faith in Action

1. Be honest now—are your words (generally) an encouragement to those who hear them (see Ephesians 4:29)?

2. Do you feel honored or ashamed when your children
   mimic the words that come out of your mouth?

3. Name three practical ways you can work on obtain-
   ing the servant's attitude of Jesus (see Philippians 2:5-
   7) while you're in the driver's seat.

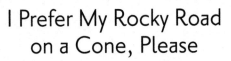

I Prefer My Rocky Road
on a Cone, Please

God's Guidance

*Start by doing what's necessary, then what's possible,
and suddenly, you are doing the impossible.*
SAINT FRANCIS OF ASSISI

*For this God is our God for ever and ever;
he will be our guide even to the end.*
PSALM 48:14, *NIV*

My daughter's puppy, Rocky, is a soul definitely in need of
guidance. He's a five-pound Russian toy terror (I mean, ter-
rier) who, when he's not incredibly adorable and cuddly, is
obtusely headstrong and self-centered. What Rocky wants
to do, Rocky does. It's a constant battle to make the little
bugger understand that he must adhere to the rules that
have been designed for his own best interests.

A purebred hunter, Rocky likes to chew, maim and destroy. It makes him happy. He indiscriminately ingests trash,
bugs and pretty flowers, regardless of toxicity level. He also
feels no inhibitions whatsoever about relieving himself
whenever and wherever the inclination moves him, and apparently suffers no remorse about ruination consequences.

But there's hope—he's young and still learning.

Rocky isn't allowed outside without his leash. After several emergency vet visits, this guideline was established to control his rocket-propelled tours of the neighborhood and input into his bottomless tummy.

No more darting in front of cars! No more nibbling poisonous toads or poinsettias! After a few test lunges, he accepts his restriction with as much dignity as can be mustered by a canine that resembles a steroidal rat.

In order to guide said pup's behavior along the path of righteousness, many doors had to close. The door to the bathroom, where he loves to redecorate the fluffy bathmat; the bedroom door, behind which he adores burrowing beneath clean bed sheets; the living room door leading to the Berber carpet he enjoys unraveling down to the nub.

The only open doors invite him to destinations previously prepared for his well-being and enrichment. His course is set by a higher authority who knows him well and understands what is best for him. Rocky has learned to adjust to his safe parameters and actually thrives within the established limitations.

I, on the other hand, attempt to rattle, dent and detach any closed door with the audacity to block my path. If the knob won't budge by brute strength, I appeal to a higher power and politely insist that God spring the lock. I pray for His will to be done. Then I proceed to inform Him what His will should be.

I decided to go to South America as a missionary; the mission board thought otherwise. I wanted to have a large family; I was blessed with two children followed by six miscarriages. I sought the highest degree in my health care profession; after two years of intensive study, I failed the final exam.

In each instance, I could hear the door hinge squeak as it slowly closed. But I was not left out in the cold.

I became a missionary in my hometown, devoted myself to nurturing the emotionally orphaned (who are all around me) and turned my energies to my writing ministry. All good things. Heart-filling things. Things that I now see were God's will for me all along.

It hasn't been until recently—watching a silly dog, of all things—that I've actually comprehended that closed doors are an integral part of God's guidance for which I've petitioned. Just as closed doors and physical restraints guide Rocky, allowing him freedom within parameters established for his good, blocked pathways in my life keep me centered on the road God has chosen for me.

Blocked pathways are not a bad thing; they're a *good* thing. So pounding on the bolted doors and trying to jimmy them open is ridiculous. They're *supposed* to be closed.

Simple, yet profound. Closed doors aren't accidental. They're not an oversight that slid by when God sneezed. They're part of the plan, even when I don't like it; even when I whine and scratch and howl because I really want what's on the other side of that insurmountable slab of wood. My job is to trust that the Closer of Doors knows me well and understands far better than I what is best for me.

It's hard for me. It's hard for you.

But there's hope—we're young and still learning.

My Savior and my God, thank You
for closing all the right doors to guide me
along the rocky road You've prepared
for me. I trust You implicitly.

Faith in Action

1. What doors have closed in your life during the last two years? Ten years?

2. Of these, which have you been tempted to pound and try to jimmy open? Why?

3. Describe a time when you prayed for God's guidance and then were disgruntled with the answer. What was His response when you told Him exactly what His will for your life should be?

37

A Sugar Addict
in a Carbo-phobic World
Nutritional Choices

Lord, help me not to ruin this fresh, new day with yesterday.
DEBORA M. COTY

*You will have plenty to eat, until you are full, and you will praise the
name of the LORD your God.*
JOEL 2:26, *NIV*

I'm sitting in a busy airline terminal. With 15 minutes left
before boarding my flight, I reach into my tote bag for a
snack. I look around. A woman from India pops grapes into
her mouth from a baggie; an earthy, long-haired couple al-
ternate bites on a banana; a woman spoons vegetable soup
from a thermos; a college student munches lean turkey on
rye; a mom distributes apple juice and spreads peanut butter on rice cakes for her kids.

I'm ashamed to scarf down the hunk of chocolate enveloped by my grubby little fingers.

Let's look at Deb's goodie stash. There's a smuggled
chocolate chip muffin from breakfast, a handful of pepper-
mints, five chocolate kisses, two PayDay candy bars, and a
bag of M&M's. Plain. The peanut ones are in my suitcase in
the belly of the airplane. Better that belly than mine.

Aside from the obvious physical ramifications of my sugar addiction, I've been lectured repeatedly by well-meaning family and friends about the dire health consequences. Yes, yes, is all I can say. I know you're right; but doggone it, I detest the taste of that healthy stuff more than a cat loathes bubble baths.

Okay, I eat salads, but only because people are watching. I consume vegetables too—when I'm shamed into it.

After 15 years of faithfully preparing squash casserole for my family, I finally had it up to my Eve's apple, burned my recipe and confessed that I abhor squash and never intend to squish a squash again. Somehow, my offspring have survived a squashless existence seemingly unscathed.

These are kids who cut their teeth on Cheese Doodly-Doos and slurped juice-flavored sugar water because we couldn't afford the real thing. Amazingly enough, they turned out to be normal, healthy people. Of course, my daughter swears she won't *ever* let me babysit *her* children until my cupboard is purged.

So what does the Bible say about food?

A little research reveals that in the beginning, before the Fall, the diet of Adam and Eve consisted of nuts, seeds and fruit (see Gen. 1:29). Not bad—even I could live with that. But after the rotten apple episode in Eden, God said, "Cursed is the ground because of you; through painful toil you will eat of it all the days of your life . . . you will eat the plants of the field. By the sweat of your brow you will eat your food until you return to the ground" (Genesis 3:17-19, *NIV*).

There it is! Do you see what I see? Part of the curse was the introduction of vegetables onto the dinner table of man! I knew it—it's our *punishment* to consume cauliflower, collards and Brussels sprouts for all our days on this earth.

But that's not all! From the time of Adam until Noah, the average lifespan was seven to eight *centuries*. Then, after the Flood, meat was added to the menu (see Genesis 9:3) and the life expectancy decreased to a handful of *decades*. Of course, drastic environmental changes came with the Flood, and I'm not blaming the current brevity of humankind's existence solely on the consumption of T-bones. No, I'm still blaming it on the nasty broccoli and turnips we eat alongside our steaks!

So what's a carbo-junkie to do in this miserable airport surrounded by health nuts? Wait—what's that I smell? Hallelujah! It's the delightfully greasy, salty aroma of French fries. I look over my shoulder to see a trim, 20-something woman caressing a Burger King bag.

Ahh. There's hope for the next generation.

Great Provider, please forgive my junk food addiction.
I confess I have a problem, and I promise to try
harder to find fulfillment in carrot sticks rather
than carrot cake. But, Lord, carrots would taste so
much better dipped in cream cheese icing . . .

Faith in Action

1. What is your stand on junk food? (Be brave—the other moms will only sneer at you for an hour or two!)

2. How do you envision your children's future feeding of their families based on your example?

3. Repeat after me: If God had wanted us to be sugar-free, He wouldn't have invented chocolate! Now go wash out your mouth with a Yoo-hoo.

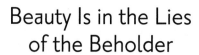

38

Beauty Is in the Lies
of the Beholder

Slaves to Fashion

Beauty is a short-lived reign.
SOCRATES

Your beauty should not come from outward adornment, such as
braided hair and the wearing of gold jewelry and fine clothes. Instead,
it should be that of your inner self, the unfading beauty of a gentle and
quiet spirit, which is of great worth in God's sight.
1 PETER 3:3-4, *NIV*

The kicker in this Scripture is the *unfading beauty* part. My
inner spirit may exude ever-vibrant beauty (you betcha!) but
what am I supposed to do with the exterior, which is fading
like a crimson sofa in the Sahara?

I've been compelled to expend considerable energy over
the years trying to make the most of my limited attributes.
But somehow I keep hitting snags. I grew my hair long in
high school and then got distracted by life. Twenty years
later, sporting waist-length locks, I won the prize at my high
school reunion for "Least Changed."

This was not a compliment.

So I tried highlighting and ended up with skunk stripes
like Cruella de Vil.

And adorning myself with clothes? I have a stunning size 6 figure. It's under there somewhere. I just keep it well padded for protection. I like to think I'm a well-rounded person. This makes the seeking of fine size 14 clothes as hard as stalking a lion on an African safari.

After mourning custard's last stand (custard pie's my favorite, but it adheres to my thighs like Polygrip) and starving myself for months on end to snag a gander at that deeply buried size 6 figure, my grumplitude blew off the charts. You know grumplitude—it's the scale of attitudinal grumpiness that fluctuates in direct relation to your: (a) blood sugar, (b) hormones and (c) sleep tank (if the tank's on E, the *fam* hauls out the big game tranquilizer dart rifle and takes cover behind the furniture).

Hoo boy, when that grumplitude volcano erupts, there are no prisoners, only casualties. "Happy wife, happy life" is but a memory.

Anyway, when the last of my targeted pounds were shed, I gleefully skipped down to Wal-Mart to buy myself a new pair of skinny jeans. Wouldn't you know, nothing was hanging on the sales rack but size 14s.

I figured I might as well buy them anyway because of the theory of Volume Relativity. VR is that phenomenon that occurs over the summer when your jeans inexplicably shrink in your dresser drawer so that when you pull them out in the fall, they're two sizes too small. (Don't bother looking up this theory in a scientific journal—it's another Coty near-fact of science.)

Then there's the Earring Paradox. Why is it that when you're shopping for a specific earring style or color, the only cute ones on the rack are clip-ons? Do people really wear those medieval torture devices nowadays? I wore them in my youthful pre-pierced days, and I still remember the agony of throbbing earlobes. Why on earth did God waste so many pain receptors on skin flaps that do nothing but droop to your shoulders to betray your age?

Do your ears hang low? Do they wobble to and fro? Can you tie 'em in a knot? Can you tie 'em in a bow? If the answer is yes, then you are likely on the north 40 (years, not property).

Fashion just ain't fair.

But then, Peter knew that. That's why he tried to save us from all the fretting, expense and frustration of adorning ourselves in the name of false beauty. The shame of not measuring up to society's unattainable standards of beauty shatters our self-esteem and makes us ungrateful for our God-given body.

No matter what size we are, we're never thin enough. But if our lips are thin, we hasten to plump them up. Straight hair must be permed. Curly hair necessitates pressing. If a forehead wrinkle appears, we starch it with Botox. We buy into the lies the mass media bombards us with, and seeds of vanity take root and grow insipidly. We heap on *more* outward adornment to make up for our perceived natural deficits.

Somewhere, sometime, somehow we must break the cycle or the cycle will eventually break us.

Jehovah-Shalom (my Peace), forgive me
when I lose sight that nurturing a gentle and quiet
spirit is infinitely of more importance than
a perfect body and matching accessories.

Faith in Action

1. Do you, too, struggle with Volume Relativity and the Earring Paradox?

2. Read 1 Peter 3:3-4. Can you pinpoint someone who exemplifies the unfading beauty of a gentle and quiet spirit? Why do you feel this way about her?

3. Do you feel pressured to adorn your outward self rather than depend on you inner beauty? Which do you think pleases God most?

A Hero Is As a Hero Does
Role Models

God interrupts our lives with His blessings.
AUTHOR UNKNOWN

Too much pride brings disgrace; humility leads to honor.
PROVERBS 29:23, CEV

My teenage hero was Amy Grant. I knew every word to every song she recorded, plastered her poster on my wall (beside David Cassidy's), and endlessly sang "My Father's Eyes" into a hairbrush. I tried to sound like her. I curled and poufed my hair to look like hers. I even fashioned a fake widow's peak in front. I wanted to *be* her.

As I matured, my heroes took on a different flavor. Oh, I'll always adore Amy Grant, but my new heroes have become everyday people who profoundly impact my life and deepen my faith. One of those heroes is a wisp of a girl whose physical size never quite caught up after her birth weight of less than two pounds.

My niece, Andie, is cerebral palsied and legally blind. My admiration for Andie can be summarized in the recounting of her first 100-meter Paralympics (competitive athletics for the physically disabled) race as a 70-pound, 13-year-old. It was a scorching Florida spring morning and the asphalt fairly sizzled on the high school track.

As the starting gun sounded, Andie threw herself forward, straining to find a rhythm for her stiff legs encased in metal braces. She worked her crutches in reciprocal patterns to balance her uneven stride.

The other runners surged ahead, leaving behind Andie and a boy who, like Andie, was unable to actually run but charged toward the finish line in a lurching walk with his wheeled walker. He was considerably larger than Andie and appeared much stronger. They were four lanes apart, but neck and neck as they neared the 50-meter mark. Total concentration was evident in both their faces as they forced their bodies to their absolute limit.

Suddenly the boy's leg brace became entangled in his walker, and he was down, face-first on the rough asphalt. A collective gasp rose from the stadium. He sprawled for only a moment and then struggled to regain his footing. The boy didn't even pause to brush the loose gravel or spattered blood from his skinned face before lunging forward once again, pushing himself harder, harder.

The crowd broke into cheers at the sheer determination of both athletes. But Andie was spent. Fatigue was evident in her posture, the way her head jutted forward to pull her dragging right leg along with every thrust of her crutches. She worked desperately, but the finite capacity of her little body was depleted.

As the two courageous warriors approached the finish line, I realized that I, like everyone else in the stands, was shouting encouragement to both athletes through tears streaming down my face. As one, we'd been deeply touched by this display of the valiance of the human spirit.

Within centimeters of the red flag, the boy edged ahead of Andie, and she staggered across the finish line in last place. But instead of being heartbroken, she was exuberant to have finished the race!

Later, at the award ceremony, Andie was surprised with the "Spirit of the Sport" award for inspiring her peers. She'd never before won a physical feat accolade. "You mean *everybody's* not getting one . . . just me?" she asked, awed by the honor. She held her trophy aloft with the unabashed joy of an Oscar winner.

"It's the biggest trophy I've ever seen," she marveled, waving before her thick glasses the standard-sized, shiny statue of a runner in mid stride. I agreed, knowing that the true magnitude of the championship isn't represented by a piece of molded plastic, but by the heart and will of its recipient.

Thankfully, heroes aren't perfect. Three of the biggest Old Testament heroes were Abraham, Isaac and Jacob. To prevent a lusty Egyptian king from murdering him to seize his gorgeous wife, Sarah, Abraham lied that she was merely his sister. Then he stood by mute as a tree trunk while the king added Sarah to his harem! Isaac showed blatant partiality to one son over the other. Jacob plotted to deceive his blind father and steal his brother's birthright.

Yet these flawed fellows are the pillars of the Judeo-Christian faith.

I find that comforting, don't you? It gives us freedom to become heroes ourselves. We driven mothers who bark, bite and devour at the worst of times, also affirm, comfort and inspire the rest of the time. *These* are the qualities our children will remember. *These* are the qualities that make us heroes.

Jehovah-Nissi (my Victorious Banner), with humility in my imperfections, I ask only to honor You in my motherhood. Make me a deserving hero to my children.

Faith in Action

1. Who is your hero?

2. Would you say this person exudes more pride or humility in her or his accomplishments?

3. As mothers, we start out as our children's greatest hero. What can we do to remain in that place of honor as they grow up?

40

Don't Knock the Flock!

Judging Others

> *The greater part of our happiness or misery depends on*
> *our disposition and not on our circumstances.*
> MARTHA WASHINGTON

> *Our Father is kind; you be kind. Don't pick on people, jump on*
> *their failures, criticize their faults—unless, of course, you want the*
> *same treatment. Don't condemn those who are down; that hardness*
> *can boomerang. Be easy on people; you'll find life a lot easier.*
> LUKE 6:36-37, *THE MESSAGE*

I'm a bit, well, shall we say—distractible. Chuck says that I'm whatever the step is beyond ADD. It's a major struggle for me to stay focused on the pastor for an entire sermon. God's shepherd has his work cut out for him keeping this ewe from straying! No matter how earthshaking the message is, my mind flits around the sanctuary like a moth on a light bulb.

It doesn't help when distractions from fellow sheep drive a worm up my nose. (I heard a sheep sermon once and it seems that sheep frequently have that worm-up-the-ol'-snoz problem.) Burrowing worms are intensely diversionary. All those little things begging for my attention—is it my fault people are so distracting?

Now, I simply can't be the *only* one with this little concentration problem in church. Anybody else out there sabotaged by these?

1. **Old Man River:** the elderly gentleman who enthusiastically belts out his deep bass voice 50 decibels LOUDer than everyone else.

2. **The Uzi Laugher:** the lady who responds to every pastoral joke with a staccato, machine-gun laugh: HA-A-A-A-A-A-A!

3. **Jolly Green Giant:** the only 6′ 8″ string bean in the church and he inevitably sits right in front of *you*. The only way to see the pulpit is to peek through Jolly's armpits.

4. **The Hoarse Whisperer:** a converser behind you using highly audible stage whispers; frequently occurs during praise songs as if they're merely the opening act.

5. **Madame Butterfly:** the operatic-voiced woman who adds an unwritten ultra-soaring soprano descant to every song.

6. **Amener:** this overly compliant person is compelled to agree with the pastor every five seconds with a resounding AMEN! Even when the pastor once remarked he had a long way to go to achieve perfection!

7. **Crinkle Chorus:** loud candy wrappers usually heard in the moment of silence immediately pre-

ceding the sermon. Why doesn't someone invent cloth wrappers for church?

8. **The Wheezer/Sneezer:** you're already seated and settled when the first juicy blast of droplet-laden air from behind blows your hair over your eyes. As one "God bless you" follows another, you can just feel the infectious bacteria swimming around your drenched neck toward your vulnerable facial orifices. Your only defense is to hike your collar like a priest and use your bulletin to deflect heat-guided germ missiles.

9. *Au Natural* **Man:** the fellow who somehow forgot to bathe this week. He enters late, sits as close to you as possible and smells like he stopped to roll in a dead possum on the way to church.

10. **Bird Nest Lady:** still wearing her teased '70s do, this short, stocky lady thinks big hair makes her look tall and thin. The only way to see around this Marge Simpson look-alike is to shift from side to side like a pendulum.

11. **Sermon Interacters:** these folks tend to grow in bunches like grapes. They like to nod a lot, point their fingers and talk back to the pastor in short, clipped sentences: "Oh, yeah!" "You said it!" "That's right!" Makes you feel like you're at a "Go, God!" pep rally.

12. **Pyrotechnic Man:** a product of the electronic era, this businessman is so important, he can't remove his cell phone for a one-hour church

service. He leaves it clipped to his belt where it distracts the entire row of people behind him by flashing vivid fireworks with each constantly incoming call. It looks like his rear end is on fire. A great object lesson for a burning bush sermon. As annoying as this is, it's less so than the fellow who neglects to turn his ringer off.

13. **Goat-Lady Singer:** this woman warbles with a choppy vibrato that sounds like a goat bleating barnyard praise. Just try to keep a straight face if your family is sitting directly in front of her. Don't even glance at your kids or you'll all end up rolling down the aisle in peals of not-so-holy hysteria. Resist the temptation to cluck or moo.

14. **Peanut Gallery:** kids old enough to know better who spend the entire service chatting to each other or their parents. Fight the impulse to rip off your pantyhose and plug their little mouths.

Okay, having said all those wicked things about my fellow sheep, I feel ba-a-a-d. I shall now beg forgiveness and respectfully ask not to be removed forcibly from the next church service. Diversity is a good thing. God never said His ewes, rams and lambs should be clones. It would be a pretty boring flock if they were. Now I just have to find myself a good nose de-wormer.

Jehovah-Rohi (God, my Shepherd), tender of wayward sheep, use Your shepherd's crook to jerk me back in line whenever necessary. Help me chill out and learn not to pick, jump and criticize my fellow sheep lest judgment boomerang back to me.

Faith in Action

1. According to Luke 6:35-37, what are four ways that we show unkindness? Which of these do you struggle with most?

2. What is the key to finding life "a lot easier"?

3. How do you handle your children's criticism or unkindness toward others?

41

Everybody Knows a Turkey
Infectious Attitudes

A closed mouth gathers no foot.
AUTHOR UNKNOWN

Sarah said, "God has brought me laughter,
and everyone who hears about this will laugh with me."
GENESIS 21:6, *NIV*

My friend Scott shares an unforgettable tale about his most memorable Thanksgiving. He was a newlywed at the time. So new, in fact, that his blushing bride, Jenna, was still trying to impress his family (and we all know how soon *that* wears off!).

In her zeal to prove her wifely worthiness, Jenna invited Scott's parents, his three married siblings and their innumerable offspring to Thanksgiving dinner, to be served at two o'clock sharp.

Scott and Jenna shopped together for the plumpest, most succulent turkey that they could find. As the big day approached, they discussed when to start defrosting the 22-pound bird. Logic dictated that it would take about 12 hours in the refrigerator. (After all, a Cornish hen required 2 hours, right?)

Just to play it safe, they transferred the rock-hard bird from the freezer to the fridge Wednesday morning, planning to get up early Thanksgiving (Thursday) and have it roasting merrily by 8:00 A.M. They slept well, with visions dancing in their heads of smiling, well-fed relatives nodding their approval.

But the next morning, plans began to plunge south. The turkey was still quite frozen and didn't respond in the least to running water. By 9:00 A.M., they had cranked the faucet hard to H and although a lovely steam bath was produced, the bird was no more pliable than a cement block. Hot air from the blow drier bounced off the impenetrable skin like spritzer off a lacquered coiffure.

Too large for the microwave, Scott had no choice but to submerge the foul fowl in a bathtub of hot water. Next came the shower massage. The turkey, which was probably very grateful for the lovely massage, was still obstinately ossified.

By 10:00, Jenna began to panic. Scott parked the bird on the kitchen counter and began pounding it with a hammer. It was like trying to drive spikes in the Arctic tundra. While Jenna dialed the Butterball hotline (yes, there *is* such a thing!), Scott decided the least he could do was remove the bag of giblets in preparation for whatever miracle the Butterball guru would impart.

He could see the giblet bag, tantalizingly close but stuck fast to the inner walls of the stubborn bird. Grabbing a knife from the drawer, he began trying to chip the stiff bag off the frozen innards. When it wouldn't budge, he marched out to the garage and returned with his toolbox. Time to play hardball.

Scott braced one foot on the edge of the counter and clinched the ornery frozen guts with his handy dandy vise grips. He pulled with all his might, teeth gnashing and head flailing, while simultaneously attacking the bird with a long-handled screwdriver.

Jenna, who'd been languishing on hold with Butterball in the bedroom, finally gained audience with a live person and entered the kitchen just in time to witness the shocking reenactment of Norman Bates' *Psycho* scene. Her bloodcurdling scream sent the Butterball lady packing and made Scott lose his grip. The turkey flew off the counter like an over-inflated football and scored a field goal through the kitchen doorway goalposts. Scott scrambled after it like a halfback recovering a fumble.

At that moment, the doorbell rang. The first wave of hungry dinner guests had arrived.

Jenna hastily mopped her eyes and ran to the door. Scott cornered the slippery raw entrée behind the potted ficus and returned it to the counter with a thud. During the lively scrimmage, the string tying the opponent's hindquarters had broken. Scott stared in disbelief at the backside of the turkey. Why, there was a huge hole between the legs of the monstrous bird! He'd been trying to wrestle the giblet packet through the neck hole!

We moms are well acquainted with planning for *perfect* family events, only to find out how outrageously *imperfect* things can turn out. It's immensely comforting to know that when there's a kink in our agenda, we can turn for help to the authority for things of eternal value—the only things that count in the end.

The Bible says that Sarah chose to laugh at one of the most unexpected, traumatic times of her life—when God announced that she would have a baby at the age of 90. She certainly wasn't planning on this twist in her future. She no doubt had a full calendar. But, bam! A sudden change of plans presented her with a fork in the road. She could either laugh or run away screeching.

She laughed.

God is there to help when we come to an unexpected fork in the road. Maybe the "fork" isn't an uncooperative turkey, but it certainly could be a rotten attitude that threatens to infect our children.

You *know* it's true: When mama ain't happy, ain't nobody happy.

So why not give 'em a break and laugh?

Lord, in Your grace, lift me higher—above the swamp, the muck and the mire! Help me remember that You may not reverse the forces of nature to solve our frozen turkey dilemmas, but You will provide grace and peace to laugh about it . . . and a deli.

Faith in Action

1. Give an example of a time when you planned the *perfect* family event, only to find out how outrageously *imperfect* things can turn out.

2. Are you able to laugh about it now? Could you then?

3. How did your attitude (at the time of the fiasco) affect your children?

42

Ain't Nothin' Like a Good Love Story

True Love

Behind every successful man is a woman who made it necessary.
BUMPER STICKER SEEN IN STARKE, FLORIDA

I love all who love me. Those who search for me will surely find me.
PROVERBS 8:17, *NLT*

Abby was frantic, agitated; some might even call her a desperate housewife. She had just received a call that would forever change her life. But then, maybe that wasn't so bad. Her life story wouldn't win any Pulitzer.

It had all seemed so promising in the beginning—10 years ago when she'd met Nabe, an ambitions college freshman intent on making a name in the business world. She'd fallen in love with his boundless energy, his lust for the good things of life. She had willingly dropped out of school to work three jobs to finance his education in pursuit of his goals . . . *their* goals.

But when it finally came to pass, when he'd ruthlessly clawed his way to the top of the financial ladder and was head of his own Fortune 500 Company, she wasn't so sure this was the life she'd bargained for. Nabe had changed. She barely saw him, and when he was home, he was always parked in front of that confounded computer or conferring with some lawyer or CEO on the phone.

Even worse, he'd gained a reputation as a financial black hole, gobbling everything in his path to satisfy his own greed. But it was never enough. He needed more, always more. The newspapers called him "The Butcher of Wall Street," and he'd insisted that everyone call him Butch, including his wife.

Abby's life seemed empty, void of meaning. At 29, she was still beautiful, but already she could see hollowness in the pale blue eyes staring back from the mirror. Could this be all there was to life . . . and love?

And then came the phone call from Carol, Butch's executive assistant, confiding that the world was about to end.

"He really did it this time; the damage is irreversible," Carol whispered, her voice tinged with fear.

"What do you mean? What did he do?" Abby asked, her stomach clinching.

"You've heard of Dave Jesseson, the CEO of Kingdom Enterprises, haven't you?"

"Well sure, who hasn't? Isn't K.E. the fastest growing conglomerate in the world?"

"That's right. It's downright miraculous how that company has exploded onto the scene. Some say God Himself must be at the helm. Anyway, it turns out that Mr. Jesseson's people have been quietly protecting some of Butch's interests from opposing companies—the ravenous wolves waiting in the wings to scarf up anything they can. Butch has no idea what a mess he'd be in if the K.E. guys hadn't interceded on his behalf." She took a deep breath.

"Just this morning, Mr. Jesseson called Butch and asked very politely if he'd be interested in forming a partnership with K.E. to develop and market a revolutionary invention to transform the livestock industry."

"What did Butch say?"

"He was rude and insulting and told Mr. Jesseson he'd made his fortune on his own and would never consider sharing any of it with the likes of him. Then he hung up on him."

"Oh, no!" Abby reached for the roll of antacid tablets she chewed like candy.

"That's not all. My friend Louise, a K.E. employee, just called to warn me that Dave Jesseson and his army of lawyers are headed over here, *as we speak,* to initiate a hostile takeover and destroy Butch. But Butch gave me strict orders not to disturb him under any circumstances. What should I do?"

Abby shook her head as the phone slid from her hand. What could anyone do? Butch was probably three sheets to the wind, drinking it up with his corporate buddies behind closed doors as he usually did on Friday afternoons.

She knew the reputation of Dave Jesseson—strong, but fair. Surely he'd listen to reason if she could just be quick enough. She flew into action, opening her home safe and filling a briefcase and two totes with her $20,000 coin collection. She grabbed Butch's half-million-dollar 1909 Honus Wagner baseball card and the 1952 Mickey Mantle worth $35,000.

Racing against time, she drove like Andretti to Butch's building, dashed through the double glass doors and across the marbled lobby where a dozen suited men were standing before the bank of elevators. Recognizing Dave Jesseson from magazine covers, Abby threw herself between him and the opening elevator door.

"Wait, please, Mr. Jesseson! I'm Butch's wife, Abby, and I beg you to hear me out."

Dave stepped back, surprise registering on his hardened, determined face.

"I know my husband has returned evil for your good, but I implore you to overlook this foolish thing he's done." She offered her valuables to him. "Please accept this humble gift and restrain from shedding corporate blood to avenge yourself. I know the Lord is with you, and I know you will never forgive yourself if you act rashly in revenge. Please forgive Butch and, most of all, forgive me for not being more aware of my husband's vile ways so I could intervene sooner."

Dave stared at her, his face softening.

"You're right," he said. "I *am* acting rashly and would most assuredly regret this act of revenge when my blood quit boiling tomorrow. Thank you for stopping me, Abby. You're quite a woman to have such presence of mind. Because of you, I won't destroy Butch. God bless and keep you, Abby."

As Dave left the building, the security guard called to inform Butch what had happened. Horrified at what had almost come to pass, Butch suffered a stroke and became as stone. Ten days later, he died.

Three weeks after the funeral, on Valentine's Day, Abby was up to her elbows sorting out the mess Butch had left her. The doorbell rang. It was a messenger bearing three dozen pink roses and a card reading, "Dearest Abby: You're as brilliant as you are gorgeous. You've won my eternal admiration. Will you be mine? Your grateful servant, Dave."

The end.

Oooh, don't you just adore a happy ending? Did you recognize the story of David and Abigail from 1 Samuel 25 (updated with a smidge of literary license)? If you found my poor rendition remotely alluring, be sure to read the original. God, who created romance, tells it best.

Lover of my soul, thank You for Your lavish, extravagant,
unending love. You truly complete me.

Faith in Action

1. Okay, girl, let it all hang out. Tell about your personal "love-of-my-life" story in glorious detail.

2. Are your cheeks rosy and your eyes twinkling? Do you feel warm and cuddly all over? Of course you do—you're feeling love as if for the first time.

3. Now let yourself comprehend that God, the Lover of your soul, feels that way about you—*all* the time. Give Him a hug.

43

Loose Change
Menopause

*You know you're having estrogen issues when you sprinkle
chocolate chips on your mashed potatoes.*
DEBORA M. COTY

*Everything on earth has its own time and its own season. . . .
There is a time for finding and losing, keeping and giving.*
ECCLESIASTES 3:1,6, CEV

As a 40-something woman, I've entered the season described
in this verse. It's called perimenopause.

I'd say the emphasis is on losing, because that seems to
be what my body and brain do best—losing car keys, sleep,
muscle tone, patience and memory. On the other hand, I've
found a few things too—10 extra pounds of insulation for
the newly acquired hot flash inferno (seems like just yesterday I was a *disco* inferno), independence as my chicks fly the
coop, and empathy with that *Saggy Baggy Elephant* I used to
read to my kids about. The only difference is he *wanted* to
grow into his baggy skin.

Fortunately, increased forgetfulness comes with a
heightened ability to laugh at myself. I recently attended an
out-of-state writer's conference, anxious to impress the dis-
tinguished publishers there.

The morning of my career make-or-break meeting, I used my curling iron sans glasses and burned a brand on my forehead in the shape of Florida. Then I discovered I'd forgotten my black heels. In fact, I'd brought no heels whatsoever. I tried to act as dignified as possible in my red and black power suit with matching forehead tattoo, gold jewelry, black clutch and ankle-high, lace-up hiking boots.

I was just waiting for someone to ask if my mama wore combat boots.

As if that wasn't humbling enough, later that night a surprise bathroom run (another thing I'm finding more of these days!) made me late in taking my seat in the ballroom where 300 attendees had assembled. Frank Peretti had already begun his keynote speech when I sashayed down the center aisle in full view of esteemed editors, renowned publishers and many of my writing heroes. Eyes turned in my direction. I held my head high, glad that I'd changed into pants so my boots weren't obvious.

As I slid into my chair, the lady beside me whispered, "Did you lose the battle?" I followed her gaze south where an eight-inch ribbon of toilet paper was stuck to the rubber sole of my hiking boot, trailing behind to flutter like a white surrender flag.

Face it, in this life the only thing that stays the same is change. And the only person who *likes* change is a baby with a wet diaper. In the vernacular of our kids, flux sucks.

During this season of change, keeping open lines of communication with Spouse is important. I've read that communication is 7 percent words, 38 percent tone of voice and 55 percent nonverbal. After decades of marital bliss, our system is honed into a fine-tuned instrument. I use as few words as possible, relying heavily on voice tone and body language.

"Nothing" when uttered in reply to his question, "What's wrong *now*?" actually means "SOMETHING!" The clue is the icy eyes, crossed arms and rivulet wrinkles pointing like tiny arrows to pencil-straight lips.

"I don't care!" with a head toss and averted eyes means, "You bet your sweet cummerbund I care!" and he knows he'd better pursue this line of questioning if he wants something other than watermelon for supper.

"Just one more minute" means 10 if pertaining to hanging up the phone, 20 if applying makeup is involved, or a literal 60 seconds if he's watching a ballgame and the trash needs to go out.

Hands on hips and a wagging chicken neck are a sure indication that "Fine!" is not a true statement when spewed at the end of an argument. It really means, "You're wrong, I'm right, and I refuse to talk about it any longer."

Heavy sigh. This is a very effective nonverbal tool when combined with eyeball rolling. It indicates patience is running thin and he needs to quickly figure out what "Nothing" is before it becomes "Fine!"

I think relinquishing my mommy role has been the hardest part of the *change*. Recently standing at a lingerie department checkout, I was mortified to hear over the store intercom, "Debbie Coty, please report to Lost and Found immediately!" Already harboring guilt about sneaking away while my 17-year-old daughter and her friend tried on clothes, I felt like an escaped convict.

As I stepped off the escalator, I heard my daughter's hysterical voice reverberating, "Moth-errrr! Where have you BEEN?" I stared speechless as she wailed with purple face and flaring nostrils, "I was SO worried! I thought you'd been KIDNAPPED!"

When did it happen? The roles had reversed. The daughter was now the nurturing worrier, and the mom the delinquent rogue. I guess I was too busy scouring toilets or chasing the prodigal dog to witness her leaping over that final crevasse of childhood.

Now I'm facing a crevasse of my own. More like a gaping ravine, really. But at least I have my hiking boots!

Restorer of my soul, during this season of change,
help me find more than I lose.

Faith in Action

1. Based on Ecclesiastes 3:1-6, in which season of life are you at the moment?

2. In which season are your children?

3. Share what you imagine the next season of your lives will encompass. How can you help them (and yourself) progress to the next phase of life as a family?

44

Adjusting Our Spiritual Antenna
Holy Spirit Whisperings

Share Christ at all times, and when necessary, use words.
ST. FRANCIS OF ASSISI

*I will ask the Father, and he will give you another Counselor, who will
never leave you. He is the Holy Spirit, who leads into all truth.*
JOHN 14:16-17, *NLT*

While pushing my cart through the paper goods aisle at
the grocery store, I was struck by the nagging notion that I
should buy extra toilet paper. *Toilet paper? Whatever for?*
And then the face of a friend popped into my head.

Julie had called the week before to ask if any of my piano students might be interested in purchasing her late
mother's heirloom piano. I knew Julie cherished the instrument she had inherited after her mother's death and
would never have considered selling it except for dire financial circumstances.

As I stood staring at the Quilted Northern, I couldn't
banish Julie's face from my thoughts. *Buy toilet paper.* The
feeling was persistent. Was God trying to tell me something?

With every moment of my busy day planned, my spiritual nature and my practical nature battled for supremacy.
It would take a good half hour to swing by Julie's house.

Could I work it in? Not really. But right there by the double-ply, the spiritual side won. Ballgames, homework and hungry kids would have to wait.

I was worried about my presumption of Julie's need as I approached her front door with several bags of groceries. What if I'd imagined a problem that didn't exist? She might be embarrassed at my act of unsolicited "charity."

Julie looked happily surprised as I toted the bags into the house and began unloading them on her kitchen table. Then without warning, she burst into tears. Startled, I turned to see her cradling the package of toilet paper like a newborn baby. Between sobs, she explained that her family had just finished their last roll and paper products had become a luxury item for their severely strained budget. She'd been collecting old newspapers to stack in the bathroom when I arrived. That toilet paper was proof positive to her that God knew and cared. He really cared!

Newspapers! I wept in my car all the way home.

Now, I'm not the sharpest scissors in the drawer, but even I recognize the hand of God when I see it. What if I hadn't listened to His still, small voice in the grocery store? What if I'd caved in to the louder voices of practicality, reason and urgency dictated by my harried life? I would have missed the phenomenal blessing of meeting someone's most rudimentary need and acting as the hands and feet of Jesus. I would have lost out because I wasn't sensitive to the Holy Spirit's promptings.

Have you met Him? The Holy Spirit, I mean. If not, please allow me to introduce you.

The Holy Spirit is the communicator of the Father, Son and Holy Spirit trinity. As a new believer, a friend once mislabeled the trinity "The Triplets," which I think really helps clarify the three-persons-in-one nature of God. The role of the Holy Spirit is to guide believers (see Acts 13:2), warn of danger (see Acts 20:23), comfort and teach us (see John 14:26), and give instruction (see Acts 1:2). How does He tell us these things?

Like radio waves broadcasting invisibly through the atmosphere, the Holy Spirit often speaks to believers. However, we must make the effort to tune in our receiver to His frequency and then choose to *obey* His guidance—even when it's inconvenient.

If my spiritual antenna isn't tuned in to these heavenly radio waves, the message may become fuzzy or garbled, and I will miss an opportunity to minister to someone as God's love with skin on it. Or maybe I cast it off as my vivid imagination or because I'm just too busy or the idea is too far-fetched to believe.

Like a gift of toilet paper.

But God has a history of sending directives that don't make sense to their recipients: Noah was asked to build a boat in a desert; Joshua was instructed to conquer impenetrable Jericho by yelling at a stone wall; Simon Peter was told he'd catch fish if he lowered his nets on the other side of the boat (duh—don't fish swim beneath the boat on *both* sides?); Mary and Martha were assured their brother was only sleeping when he'd been deader than a fencepost for four days.

Whether the Holy Spirit speaks through inner urgings, persistent thoughts, church sermons, Christian friends, or via Scripture sharper than a two-edged sword, He is trying to get through to us. His job is to intercede as our Helper in living a victorious Christian life.

Even if He has to whisper behind the squeezable Charmin.

*Gracious Father, Son of Man and Holy Spirit,
never stop whispering to me! Hit me between the
eyes when necessary. Guide me. Teach me. Use me
as your go-to girl in helping others.*

Faith in Action

1. What is your personal experience with the Holy Spirit?

2. To which of the roles of this member of "The Triplets" are you most attuned (see John 14:26; Acts 1:2;
   13:2; 20:23)?

3. Would you like to be more tuned in to the whisper-
   ings of the Holy Spirit? Brainstorm three ways to adjust your spiritual antenna for better reception.

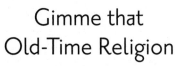

45

Gimme that
Old-Time Religion

Trust

It's easier to preach 10 sermons than it is to live one.
AUTHOR UNKNOWN

*I know that you sincerely trust the Lord, for you have the faith of your
mother, Eunice, and your grandmother, Lois.*
2 TIMOTHY 1:5, *NLT*

It was an overcast Sunday morning in late October. The
Smoky Mountains mist was bone-chilling at our remote
vacation cabin as my family bundled up and filed outside
to our car. Chuck flipped on the heater to muzzle the bite
of frosty air.

Heading over the river and through the woods to
church, we suddenly found the twisting mountain road
blocked by a barricade and sign proclaiming "Bridge Closed
for Repairs." As Chuck turned the car around, I spotted a
weathered church sign peeking through the weeds. With no
better idea (except the kids' suggestion to return to the
cabin and meditate on the warmth of our beds), we decided
to give it a try.

Turning off the main road, we ascended a hill toward a
steeple-topped country church bordered by an enormous

hickory tree on one side, a centuries-old cemetery on the other and a drafty outhouse in back. As we timidly climbed the wooden steps, we were greeted by surprised smiles and warm handshakes as if we were the only visitors that little sanctuary had seen in a long while.

My family sat on a polished wooden pew as the choir (which turned out to be all 15 members of the congregation) gathered around an old upright piano in the corner. God's presence filled that place as the off-key choir joyfully and robustly brought in the sheaves, leaned on the everlasting arms and claimed their place in line when the roll is called up yonder. (I could swear one grinning grandpa warbled, "When the rolls are served up yonder, I'll be there!")

I felt like I'd stepped back in time. A tear tickled my nose when they launched into my long-deceased grandmother's favorite, "The Church in the Wildwood."

I doubted many of the worshipers in my super-sized, urbanized church at home had ever heard those beloved old hymns, much less felt their hearts transported to God's throne by a group of mountain folk in their best frocks and overalls. For me, it was truly an unexpected slice of heaven.

Then, when I thought my spiritual temperature could climb no higher without bursting my heart right out of my chest, a strapping young man who doubled as a farmer during the week and preacher on Sundays strode purposefully to the pulpit. He preached a rousing sermon encouraging his flock to "Walk close to the Lord," complete with an unforgettable illustration that went something like this:

"When I was a boy, my daddy used to take me coon huntin' after dark. Some nights, them woods were pitch-black, and Daddy would walk in front of me to blaze a trail. As long as I was right behind him, followin' in his footsteps,

I was protected. But the minute I commenced to daydream and fall away from the path he made for me . . . whack! A low branch he'd pushed aside would pop back in my face and slap the snot outta me.

"Followin' our heavenly Father is the same way. If we don't stay close and follow directly in His footsteps, we'd best watch out! We're gonna get the snot knocked outta us by the devilish tree limbs of life coming at us from the dark."

Well now, I think that gifted country preacher translated a profound spiritual truth into the best analogy I've ever heard. I can think of many times I've lagged behind my heavenly Father's footsteps and had the snot slapped out of me by life's tree branches flying out of nowhere: overwhelming debt (from spending my money in the wrong places), misunderstandings (when I allowed my rogue tongue to run wild), running late (because of poor choices and irresponsible use of my time) and alienating dear friends (due to my overly critical spirit).

The wonderful thing about our heavenly Father is that He doesn't hold it against us when we stray from His path and stumble around in the dark woods. He welcomes us back to His side with His flashlight of forgiveness and never quits blazing the trail just before us.

> *Father God, I want to stay close to You always, walking in Your footsteps. When I stray, knock the snot outta me with those tree limbs so I will always remember my safety is in Your shadow.*

Faith in Action

1. Do you have a legacy of faith in your family like Timothy (see 2 Timothy 1:5)?

2. Regardless of your past, name five ways you can create a legacy of faith for your children and grandchildren.

3. Do you feel that you're walking closely enough in the Lord's footsteps to avoid the devilish tree limbs of life slapping the snot out of you? What are two ways you can ensure a closer walk to benefit from the safety of His shadow?

Poxes on Those Little Foxes

Intimacy

A happy marriage is the triumph of imagination over irritation.
DEBORA M. COTY

Quick! Catch all the little foxes before they ruin the vineyard of your love,
for the grapevines are all in blossom.
SONG OF SONGS, 2:15, *NLT*

In Solomon's day, grapes were a big deal. Productive vineyards were bread and butter, the family business, the means by which to buy a stunning new toga and sandals. When wild critters snuck in and ravaged the plants, the family's wellbeing was severely damaged or even ruined for good.

Solomon, wise guy that he was, cleverly compared the destructive foxes he daily eradicated from his vineyards to the troublesome relationship-eroding vexations plaguing his marriage. Yep, it's those pesky *little* foxes that can wreck havoc on our vineyards of love. You know what I mean: the annoying habits, quirks and nuances that, over time, irritate the pedubies out of your spouse.

I'm not talking big, hunky elephant-sized differences like worldview, political preferences or choice of financial investments. I mean itty-bitty disagreements like which end to squeeze the toothpaste tube, hanging the toilet paper flap up or down (not to mention the seat!) and the prefer-ence of paper over plastic.

Then there's the cleavage index. No, not the size of your chest; cleavage as in *cleaving* (joining, holding on to). Eph-esians 5:31 tells us, "For this cause [marriage] shall a man leave his father and his mother, and shall cleave to his wife; and the two shall become one flesh" (*ASV*). If either spouse can't leave and cleave, snip the apron strings with mom or dad and make his or her life partner the most important person, a whole pack of cunning little foxes will bust right through the fence and rip into those grapevines.

My friend Gracie was routinely ignored while her hus-band, Mark, spent one to two hours daily on the phone with his widowed mother. Family activities, dinner and couple time with Gracie took a backseat. A low cleavage index threw a *big, fat* fox into their marital vineyard. To catch the wily creature, Mark had to learn to set limits and repeat the phrase, "I love you, Mom, but this is not a good time; can I call you back later?"

I've come to realize every marriage is full of nasty little foxes hiding in the shadows, just waiting to sabotage spousal intimacy.

Chuck and I met under idyllic circumstances in the 1970s, on a college campus—me, a hick from the Southern sticks, and he, a displaced yankee from New York. I thought the way he strummed his guitar was "groovy, far out, man," and he thought it charming the way I made two syllables out of words like "door" and "pen."

We've never been one of those palsy-walsy couples who do everything together, but we do enjoy mutual accomplish-ments. Despite our personality differences, we've learned to shoo the fox cubs out of our den before they start to grow.

Take home projects, for example. We discovered during the early years of our marriage that we could do home projects together, but not simultaneously. Our polar opposite ways of doing things often resulted in critical attitudes, bossiness and wounded feelings.

I'm a just-get-it-done-as-quickly-as-possible person, and he's a take-your-time, every-detail-counts guy. I say quantity; he says quality. So we worked out a system.

I slap a strip of wallpaper on the walls and leave the room. He enters and methodically does all the precision trimming. Repeat process until room is completed. We then return hand-in-hand and proudly congratulate each other on a job well done.

He starts the fruit salad by carefully slicing a fresh pineapple into perfect, half-inch cubes. I finish by tossing in whatever I can find—apples, strawberries, tomatoes, onions (aren't onions fruit?)—chopped willy-nilly into strange geometric shapes sporting bits of peel clinging to their backs. The results? Delicious!

Could our contrasting attributes become irritating little foxes? You betcha.

Yet love is a many-splintered thing. God often chooses to bring "odd couples" like us together, and the only way to send those relationship-infiltrating foxes packing is to follow the Manufacturer's instructions:

Love is kind and patient, never jealous, boastful, proud, or rude. Love isn't selfish or quick tempered. It doesn't keep a record of wrongs that others do. Love rejoices in the truth, but not in evil. Love is always supportive, loyal, hopeful, and trusting. Love never fails (1 Corinthians 13:4-8, *CEV*)!

Merciful Lord, like Solomon, I'm grateful that You chose my beloved just for me. Give my sneakers wings to catch those sneaky little foxes threatening to ruin my vineyard. Send the damaging dudes fox trotting far away from my juicy grapevines of love.

Faith in Action

1. What is the security status of your vineyard of love?

2. Name three of the "little foxes" that threaten your grapevines.

3. What are some creative ways you can trap those sneaky little foxes and protect your beautiful vineyard blossoms? (A good place to start is 1 Corinthians 13:4-8.)

47

Cooking Up Joy
Culinary Adventures

*A woman is like a teabag; you never know how strong
she is until she gets in hot water.*
NANCY REAGAN

Our mouths were filled with laughter, our tongues with songs of joy.
PSALM 126:2, *NIV*

When it comes to cooking, I'm a real disappointment to my mother, one of the top 10 cooks in the Deep South.

Mama spends all day preparing dinner, which is incomplete without meat (she often has poor Daddy supervising spit-rotated pork roasting in the back yard), at least two vegetables (one green, one yellow for color balance), her famous mashed potatoes (more like a preview of heaven than a vegetable), bread with creamy butter, homemade strawberry jam and stewed tomatoes. Then there's congealed salad (this isn't considered fruit, salad or dessert, although it's a conglomeration of all three), "real" salad (mixed greens/carrot salad/three-bean salad), fresh fruit bowl and relish tray (an artful display of homemade pickles, relishes and deviled eggs). Oh, and don't forget the smorgasbord of freshly baked pies and cakes (Mama considers it tacky if there's not a choice of at least three).

Excuse me while I wipe the dripping saliva off my manuscript.

I, however, am a dump cook. No, I didn't say *dumb* cook, although some may beg to differ when I substitute salt if I'm out of sugar (hey, it's white and granular!). For the sake of saving time, energy and dishwashing, I dump everything together in one dish—meat, vegetables, starch and, oftentimes bread (a little soggy, but not problematic for those who sop up their pot liquor anyway).

I've even been known to throw in a little fruit from time to time to camouflage the taste of the vegetables.

One of my more memorable efforts was spinach-mango pizza. Sure seemed like a good idea. The kids retched. The dog wouldn't even eat it. We had to bury it in the backyard under the azalea bushes. Poor suckers withered like I'd marinated them in lemon juice.

However, I've been fortunate enough to discover the mystical, magical secret to perfect cooking every time. Are you ready? You will want to share this with all your domesticated friends. Here it is: *cheese.* Yes, CHEESE: The Culinary Cure-All. If the food's undercooked, melt some mozzarella on top to hold it together. Overcooked? Just scrape off the black and slap on sharp cheddar to disguise the burnt taste. Tough as a saddlehorn? Chop it up and drown it in Cheese Whiz. Too runny? Sprinkle in a fistful of Monterey Jack and call it bisque.

Like a bubble bath for achy arches and ice cubes for boo-boos, cheese will fix anything.

My one consolation is that as anemic as my culinary prowess is, my sister Heather's is worse. When you eat at Heather's house, you'll be served the same fare whether the Pope or Big Daddy Weave is dining: hamburgers and hotdogs.

Now, these aren't just your run-of-the-mill burgers and dogs. The burgers are black, hard, hockey-puck things that have totally lost any resemblance to the ground beef patties from whence they came. They now look more like the cow patties we threw as childhood Frisbees. We affectionately call them puckburgers.

And the weenies! I used one rubber dog to plug a pot-hole in the driveway.

It's amusing to watch someone eat at Heather's house for the first time. The smiling guest innocently goes to the counter to load his bun (which Heather has attempted to toast in the oven, succeeding only in morphing it into a black-bottomed brick). After repeatedly stabbing his fork at an unyielding puckburger, he ends up politely sliding it onto his bun.

On goes a little mayonnaise and ketchup, maybe a dab of mustard.

He sits and takes his first bite. The smile fades. Next thing you know, he's back at the counter adding a big old hunky slice of tomato, a dozen lettuce leaves and half an onion. Another bite. The bun lid comes off.

He adds a scoop of baked beans, right on top, then a handful of potato chips. By the time dinner's halfway over, he's got that bun piled high with everything on the table—a couple deviled eggs smashed on there, a wedge of can-taloupe and tangerine congealed salad oozing out the sides.

Thankfully, Heather laughs along with me about our cooking misadventures. We've learned that laughter is a nat-ural medicine—a tremendous stress reliever, the zipper we pull to let that ol' bottled up tension come spilling out.

And it's *so* much cheaper than smashing Pyrex against the wall!

*Glorious Creator, when my creations flop, fill my
mouth with laughter instead of curses, and my tongue
with joyful noises instead of complaints.*

Faith in Action

1. All modesty aside, rate your cooking skills on a 1 to
   10 scale (1 = poor, 10 = outstanding). Either way, do
   you have a sense of humor about it? Why or why not?

2. How much of your culinary ability was influenced by
   your mother? Your grandmother?

3. Many women feel that preparing food for their families is an act of love. Do you feel this way?

48

Passing the Test

Perseverance

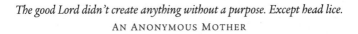

The good Lord didn't create anything without a purpose. Except head lice.
AN ANONYMOUS MOTHER

Blessed is the man who perseveres under trial, because when he has stood the test, he will receive the crown of life that God has promised to those who love him.
JAMES 1:12, NIV

One of God's missionaries to Coty-land was Ernest P. Squirrel, the intended brunch of a hungry cat. As an infant, Ernest escaped the drooling jaws of death and shimmied up my leg (which apparently resembles a tree trunk) for protection. I fed him every two hours with an eyedropper and—ironically—cat's milk until he achieved release-into-the-backyard status. (Did you know that cat's milk comes in handy juice boxes? I assume this is for discerning kittens' lunch boxes.)

Having been raised by humans, Ernest was not up to snuff in Basic Squirrel Skills 101, like springing from limb to limb in the canopy of oak trees surrounding our house. I witnessed one ill-fated attempt when his groping front paws missed the target limb. He sailed downward, unceremoniously crashing through leaves until he hit the ground.

Thud.

As I frantically considered how one might perform rodent CPR, he sat up, looked unsteadily around and then scrambled back up the tree to try again. *Try again* was his motto, as he proved when failing other squirrel proficiency tests like climbing the greased bird feeder pole, or searching for lost acorns he'd stashed away (how I wish I could find *half* the goodies I've stashed "in a safe place").

Yes, Ernest was a role model in perseverance. He didn't complain; he didn't throw his paws into the air and give up; he didn't even cop a rotten attitude and stomp around throwing pinecones. He tackled his trials head-on with quiet determination. And because of that attitude, he learned and grew.

We've all been through times of trial. I suspect we can all recall times when our endurance faltered. My driest desert was the depression surrounding six heart-wrenching miscarriages. I yearned for God's refreshing stream in a parched land as my faith choked and trust withered. I couldn't pray. I couldn't go to church. I felt abandoned, lost, hopeless.

Out of sheer desperation, I began reading the psalms—not the exalting, worship-filled psalms, but the *scream-at-God* kind, like chapters 6, 22, 42, 44, 55, 69, 74, 77, 102 and 143. David's words of despair became my prayers. They were a balm to my scorched spirit. Eventually, I progressed to the *help-me-trust-again* chapters like 4, 18, 25, 30, 34, 37, 56, 63, 121 and 139. And gradually, through much prayer and healing, I was able to once again praise my heavenly Father through passages like Psalms 3, 9, 20, 73, 84, 91, 96, 100, 116 and 147.

I tentatively shared my experience and found support from Christian sisters who had persevered through personal deserts and strode out the other side with faith stronger than before. I know it won't be my last trip to the spiritual desert. That vast wasteland lurks behind every dream-shattering loss and deep disappointment in life. But our time there diminishes with each visit as our trust in God grows more resilient.

You may feel burning sand between your toes right now. When you're trudging through, the spiritual desert feels like a lonely, barren expanse that will never end. Many times you can't lift your weary head enough to see your next step, much less the rising sun on the horizon.

But it *is* rising and you're not alone. There is hope. Many others, including the psalmist David, have endured the arid desert path and reached the oasis on the other side. His words are recorded in the Bible to help you. Try progressively praying the psalms as I've described and tell God exactly how you feel. He can take your angry words. You can even beat on His chest and cry. He's a BIG God. It's through His strength that we can try, try again.

I once read that persecuted European Christians don't pray like American Christians—for God to lessen their loads. They pray for stronger backs.

Ever-loving Lord, You are as rivers of water in a dry place [see Isaiah 32:2]. Help me realize that I am not alone in my desert. Lead me to reach out for help to persevere. And Father, please strengthen my back.

Faith in Action

1. What source of strength do you turn to during times of trial?

2. Read Psalm 22. Can you feel David's desperation and anger at God? Now read Psalm 55. What was David's attitude toward the Lord in this Scripture?

3. Mark these passages in your Bible so that you can return to them when your spirit is in a desert place.

He's Got My Goat

Redemption

Humor is the prelude to faith, and laughter is the beginning of prayer.
REINHOLD NIEBUHR

*All of us were like sheep that had wandered off. We had each gone our own
way, but the LORD gave him [Jesus] the punishment we deserved.*
ISAIAH 53:6, CEV

I feel sure that when Isaiah penned these words, he would have had no problem including goats with the sheep in the livestock analogy. This slight variation is important to me, for recent events have illustrated to me that I, quite frankly, am a goat.

It was a breezy spring morning and the sweet scent of orange blossoms perfumed the Florida air. I was playing tennis—doubles—with three friends at a rural tennis club. The court we occupied was flanked by open fields subdivided by a wire fence. The pasture adjacent to the tennis court contained a herd of goats, many of which had become like squat, smelly friends to us from their long-term tennis spectatorship and were, we fancied, our biggest fans.

On this particular day, the far field, usually vacant, was home to an ill-tempered, pernicious donkey that wasn't about to *take no "gruff"* from the insubordinate goats who liked nothing better than to pester her. She had, in fact, previously dispatched one to goat heaven via her sharp hooves, hence the separate quarters.

If all parties had only acknowledged that their all-wise master knew what was best and subsequently honored his painstaking arrangements, all would have been rosy. But no, there was a rebel in paradise. Hershey (my name for the white goat that looked like someone had held him up by his hind hooves and dipped his front half in a vat of chocolate) stubbornly refused to acknowledge the parameters placed upon him and shimmied beneath the wire fence to the forbidden domain of the donkey.

Well, that ornery donkey was having none of the trespasser and lit off after him like a greyhound after a rabbit. Around the pasture they ran, Hershey desperately using fallen trees and mounds of debris as an obstacle course to elude his pursuer. But the donkey stayed right behind him, dogging him over and around all deterrents to achieve her all-consuming goal—the demise of said goat.

At first we humans were amused by this new sport. Then Hershey began to tire and lagged enough that the donkey's lips curled back and her rack of large teeth protruded to take a furry plug out of the terrified goat's hindquarters.

Kendy, the animal-lover (who calls a "let" to usher misguided inchworms off the tennis court), leapt into action. Catapulting over the fence, she raced into the field, snatching a leafless branch from a pile of wood to wield over her head like a battle-ax. She fell in line behind the donkey screaming, "Whoa! Whoa there, you!" Then the donkey got *really* mad. HEE-HAWing and snorting, her devilish eyes rolled back at Kendy in a most threatening manner, causing those of us lining the fence to holler to our friend to get out of there posthaste before she became hoof fodder.

But desist she would not, so a ridiculous parade ensued—
Kendy chasing the donkey that was chasing the goat round
and round the field like a bizarre Three Stooges episode.

Finally, another tennis player gathered enough wits to
open the gate and yell, "Here, goatie . . ." Kendy caught on
and herded the tenacious stampede in that direction. Hershey bee-lined for the escape route, officially becoming the
'scape goat and left the donkey stomping and braying her
displeasure. Kendy took advantage of this impromptu ora-
tory and hurdled over the fence.

When I stopped laughing, God, as usual, used this object lesson to address a recurrent issue in my life: cheating. I
routinely fudge when playing games, even with my children
(I simply *must* win!); sneak goodies on my diet (if no one sees
me it doesn't count, right?); and talk myself into "borrow-
ing" small items from work (they have a gazillion of them!).

I've become the queen of justification.

But what if, while convincing myself it's no big deal
and desensitizing myself through repetition, my cheating
escalated to a more catastrophic scale . . . like my marriage? If I'm not honest in little things, will I be honest in
big things?

The Bible draws a parallel with the integrity we exhibit
in small versus large responsibilities. "You have been faithful with a few things; I will put you in charge of many
things" (Matthew 25:21, *NIV*). God sees and rewards those
who reflect His nature in even the tiniest ways.

So I need to view setting an honest example for my children as no small responsibility. Sin is sin, no matter the size.
If it matters to God, it should matter to me.

Like Hershey the 'scape goat, I often disregard the
boundaries God, my master, has placed for my own protec-

tion through His Word. Why? Because it's exciting! It's ever so much more invigorating to flirt with danger than hang out in the pasture picking dandelions.

But excitement quickly fades. Once I've snuck into the off-limits territory, that ol' devilish donkey relentlessly pursues me until I suffer spiritual wounds beneath the sharp hooves of my sin's consequences.

My daughter's innocent face falls as she loses yet another Rummy game. Those smuggled brownies don't make me feel better; they make me feel fat. Stealing is stealing. Plain and simple.

God's Son has mercifully rescued me from my just and deserved fate—like Kendy, who jumped in to save the foolish goat that, without her intervention, was headed for utter disaster. Jesus willingly accepted my punishment—death—and bought me freedom and forgiveness for my sin.

I thank God that He's got my goat.

Great Protector, when I wander into dangerous pastures of temptation, make me mindful of the sacrifice You made to rescue prodigal goats like me.

Faith in Action

1. Who does the goat represent in this chapter? What are the ways in which you typically sneak past your boundaries?

2. Who is a metaphor for Jesus? Explain why.

3. How can 1 Corinthians 10:13 help you to overcome your temptations?

Keeping Christ in Christian Holidays

Celebrating Christ

My mother didn't tell me how to live; she showed me.
AUTHOR UNKNOWN

We will not hide these truths from our children but will tell the next generation about the glorious deeds of the LORD. We will tell of his power and the mighty miracles he did. . . . So each generation can set its hope anew on God.
PSALM 78:4,7, NLT

"Now, walk Jesus down the road lined with toothpicks, but be careful not to let Him fall off Battlecat!"

"Okay, but if G. I. Joe is playing Peter, can he bivouac behind the couch after the rooster crows?"

"Mommy, can Skeletor be Pontius Pilate?"

"Hey! You're supposed to throw the palmetto fronds in the road for Jesus, *not* poke your sister with them!"

"We don't have enough twist ties to hold both Ken dolls on the crosses beside Jesus. Oops—the pencil lead just broke and the cross fell off the shoe box of Calvary!"

"Oh, no! The dog's chewing up Judas and the 30 pieces of tin foil!"

Bizarre as these comments sound, they were part of our Easter tradition as my children grew up. In order to make the Easter story more real to them, we acted out the entire week preceding Easter with dolls, beginning with Jesus' Palm Sunday entry into Jerusalem and ending with His glorious resurrection.

We had a real Jesus doll I'd purchased at a Christian bookstore, but the rest of the cast was assembled (with a lot of imagination) from the toy box. That first year, He-Man was in vogue, so he and his trusty green tiger-steed, Battlecat, and SheRa and their adversary, Skeletor, had starring roles, along with the Barbie gang and army guys in full regalia.

On Good Friday, we'd set aside an hour to open up the big picture Bible and gather our props, which included three crosses made of pencils rubber-banded together and stuck point-down into a sturdy shoe box. The box also doubled as Jesus' tomb, so that when we completed the story up to the crucifixion, the crosses were removed. Jesus was wrapped carefully in a shroud of tissue and buried in the shoe box cave with a round pillow rolled in front of the opening.

We placed the box by the fireplace and tiptoed reverently around it until Jesus sprang forth from the grave on Easter morning. My college-age offspring still talk about how exciting it was to awaken early and run into the living room to find the tissue grave clothes discarded in a pile and Jesus miraculously sitting atop the shoebox tomb in his purple robe, his little plastic arms raised triumphantly in the air.

Corny, you may say. But the kids loved this symbolic ritual honoring our Lord Jesus, and it served to imprint these most important events, crucial to our faith, in their minds forever. And what a fun way to energize the Easter message!

For creative moms, there are all kinds of ways to keep Christ in Christian holidays! For the noncreative (like *moi*), just copy somebody else!

I copied a friend's birthday cake for Jesus at Christmas. The chocolate cake symbolized our sins; the white icing, Jesus' purity covering our sins. Red candles forming a cross stood for Jesus' freely spilled blood to offer us everlasting life (signified by sprigs of evergreen around the base of the cake). My creative contribution was to scootch our manger scene angel into the cake (I fancied that she'd enjoy having her feet immersed in chocolate as much as I would).

Another friend hung a Christmas stocking for Jesus, and each family member wrote down something they'd done in Jesus' name that year—saved money for missions, invited a friend to church, learned six Bible verses, even "helped Mom around the house more" (don't you wish!). Then they opened Jesus' stocking first on Christmas morning and shared his "gifts" before tearing into their own.

My friend Gloria created a family tradition of Gospel Easter Eggs. Each year, she'd invite neighborhood children to join her own three daughters to read the story of Jeremy, a mentally handicapped boy who—unlike his friends who were focused on candy, gifts and bunnies—recognized the true meaning of Easter by an empty Easter egg (the egg was empty just like Jesus' tomb!).

Gloria hid plastic eggs filled with other mementos of Easter: flowers symbolizing new life; tiny nails for Jesus giving His life on the cross for us; a dirty rag representing sin; 30 cents signifying the silver paid to Judas. You get the idea. And so did the kids. Many learned about God's Son for the first time at this much anticipated neighborhood event.

Although she's not Jewish, Marianne wanted her children to respect the Jewish customs in which Jesus participated, so she established an annual family Passover Dinner (Seder) held on Good Friday. Using books from the Christian bookstore and those published by Jews for Jesus, they performed the ancient ceremony, pointing out symbolism of various facets of Christianity as well as Judaism. This tradition now includes Marianne's nine grandchildren.

> *Light of the world, and our lives, reflect through us*
> *as we share our faith with future generations through*
> *traditions we create with our children today.*

Faith in Action

1. Name one family holiday tradition you've established that reflects your Christian values.

2. Can you think of two other Christ-centered family traditions that are effectively implemented by friends? Have you ever considered doing them in your home? What stops you?

3. What family traditions do you think are so meaningful to your children that they'll want to pass them on to their children "so each generation can set its hope anew on God" (Psalm 78:7, *NLT*)?

Sweetest Dreamzzzz
Sleep Deprivation

Pampered women don't have an extra chin. They cream them
away or pat the muscles until they become firm. But this chin has
always been there, supporting a nodding head that has slept in a
chair all night . . . bent over . . . praying.
ERMA BOMBECK

Come to me, all you who are weary and burdened, and I will give you rest.
MATTHEW 11:28, *NIV*

As a sleep-deprived mother, I yearned for that rapturous
rest, but it was terribly illusive. I took comfort in knowing
that God provides a special verse for mothers: "So then, let
us not be like others, who are asleep, but let us be alert and
self-controlled" (1 Thessalonians 5:6, *NIV*). And I don't have
to tell you, sister, without God's intervention, self-control is
a scarce commodity at 3:00 A.M.

There's nothing quite so stirring as a newly awakened
mother first thing in the morning, trying to crack open her
swollen eyelids enough to tell if she is truly combing her
hair with her toothbrush. The image in the mirror reflects
incredulity as she decides if those dark smudges under her
eyes could be grape jam stains from yesterday's lunch.

After endless hours identifying with the fabled princess
and that pesky pea, I've concluded that we mothers experience four phases of sleep:

1. **Preparation:** One assumes the correct position (horizontal), although the brain and body are still in a fully functioning mode of operation. The muscles are tense and the mind continues to race over mountains of unfinished chores, suddenly remembered grocery necessities and errands long deferred. The perpetual hope is that a miracle will occur and rigidity will suddenly be replaced by the velvety black blanket of unconsciousness.

2. **The Zombie Zone:** Physical exhaustion from tossing and turning eventually results in muscular relaxation, although mental alertness continues. Endless "to do" lists parade through the brain, like sheep wearing little electronic sign boards flashing reminders like: *Check the breakfast milk for chunks before pouring.*

3. **La-La Land:** This is the period of physical and mental fogginess—that place where you're not quite asleep, but not awake either. This phase can also be a "You-can't-touch-me-with-your-whining!" state of oblivion. You simply block out the cacophony of sounds that threaten to envelope you . . . like having a pillow over your head during a sandstorm. Muffled chaos becomes tolerable chaos.

4. **Blissful Unconsciousness:** This phase is too often brief but incredibly refreshing. It can be reached as a transition from Phase 3 or achieved

unexpectedly by sitting on a sofa in the late afternoon. Side effects may include an interesting
maze of facial furrows from the pile of unfolded
laundry upon which your head lands.

While in the grocery store checkout line, I overheard a
revealing conversation between two young mothers. One
was draped over the handle of her cart, head propped on her
hand, with a whimpering baby in a car seat and a hyperac-
tive toddler tossing a package of cheese riddled with tooth
marks at the cashier's head.

Turning to the woman behind her, who was balancing a
baby on one hip and a jumbo pack of diapers on the other,
she pointed to a tabloid magazine headline heralding, "Man
Awakens from 30-year Sleep."

"Doesn't that sound heavenly?" the drooping mom
asked wistfully.

"Ooooh, yeah!" the other woman emphatically replied.

So how can we enhance those precious but few oppor-
tunities we do have to sleep? The following are a few techniques I've found helpful.

Develop a routine. Sleep in a designated spot at a designated time. Routine is important for tipping off your body
that it's time to close up shop instead of building a new one.

Wind down. Discipline yourself to do something relaxing before bedtime, whether that is soaking in a warm bubble bath or sipping a cup of hot herbal tea (just remember,
no caffeine)!

Regular exercise (running after the kids doesn't count) is
beneficial for inducing sleep at night. A brisk walk with the
stroller, using a home fitness machine or a favorite exercise
video are excellent ways of cleaning out the mental cobwebs

and simultaneously doing something good for you. Don't exercise at least three hours before bedtime or you may be stirring up the fire instead of dousing the embers.

Avoid using the bed as your worktable. Condition yourself to use the bed for sleeping, so the mind will turn itself off at the desired time and place.

White noise can help lull you into mental dullness. Soft, steady tones will avoid drowning out the sound of nighttime emergencies. A fan works, if you aren't in northern Wisconsin in January, or my favorite, a droning air purifier.

Pass the Parchment. Write down all those to-dos so you don't have to remember them. It relieves stress immensely to turn off those brain circuits and turn over the job of recollection to the mighty pen. Keep a pad by your bedside to jot down anything important that pops into your brain when dozing off.

Cuddle something. After pouring out consolation and reassurance to little people all day, it refills your own emotional teapot to receive physical reaffirmation. If available, a husband is a delightful source of soothing touch, as long as he understands that SLEEP is the end goal. A special stuffed animal or soft blanket (yes, adults have binkies too!) can help calm frazzled nerves.

Meditate on God's Word. Reflecting on a favorite verse is a wonderful way to bring peace and relaxation to your soul. One of my midnight favorites is Proverbs 3:5-6: "Trust in the LORD with all your heart and lean not on your own understanding; in all your ways acknowledge him, and he will make your paths straight" (*NIV*). Another scripture that calms the savage beast within is Matthew 11:29: "Take my yoke upon you and learn from me, for I am gentle and humble in heart, and you will find rest for your souls" (*NIV*).

If all else fails, remember that you're not alone—mothers have functioned in the same sleep-deprived state for thousands of years and have not only survived but lived productive lives that honor God. We are a sisterhood of slightly sagging spiritual warriors. But, as God reminds us, "My grace is sufficient for you, for my power is made perfect in weakness" (2 Corinthians 12:9, *NIV*).[1]

> *Dear God of all comfort, help me to not forget that the sweetest rest comes when I am secure in Your love and ability to take care of me. "I will lie down and sleep in peace, for you alone, O LORD, make me dwell in safety" [Psalm 4:8, NIV].*

Faith in Action

1. In which phase of sleep (as described in this chapter) do you spend most of your allocated rest time?

2. Brainstorm three sleep-inducing techniques you're willing to try to avoid another sleepless night.

3. Which meaningful Scripture would you be most likely to meditate on when sleep eludes you? (You may use one of the passages in this chapter or another of your favorites.)

Note
1. Excerpts taken from "Sweetest Dreamzzzz" by Debora M. Coty, first appearing in the September/October 2005 issue of *MomSense*. Used by permission.

I Fought the Lawd, and the Lawd Won

Submission

There's a time to submit, and there's a time to outwit.
RUTH GRAHAM

*God is with us; he is our leader. . . . Do not fight against the LORD, the
God of your fathers, for you will not succeed.*
2 CHRONICLES 13:12, *NIV*

People sometimes wonder why there's a page torn from my Bible. Yep, it's ripped right out. The passage containing 1 Peter 2–3 is folded and tucked neatly between the pages. I keep it there to remind me of the battle I waged—and lost—with God.

Brace yourself, girl, it's time to talk about that dreaded, misunderstood, miscommunicated word: "submission" (*grimace*). After nearly 30 years of marriage, this is a subject about which I am still in the learning process.

As a young adult, I prided myself on my independent thinking (I can do *any*thing), emotional insulation ("No woman is an island" doesn't apply to me!), and tolerance of the inferior sex (men). I was quite sure that women, although perhaps not physically stronger, were stronger mentally, spiritually, emotionally and certainly had better manners. I was my own decision maker, rarely asking for input from anyone (except maybe which antifungal foot spray to buy).

As a newly married woman, I rued passages like Ephesians 5:22-24: "You wives will submit to your husbands as you do to the Lord. For a husband is the head of his wife as Christ is head of his body, the church; he gave his life to be her Savior. As the church submits to Christ, so you wives must submit to your husbands in everything" (*NLT*).

I argued long hours with my pastor about what I saw as the inequality of women's marital submission to man. After all, I protested, shouldn't the best qualified have the last word, regardless of gender? God doesn't differentiate between the sexes—He loves us all equally. So shouldn't we have equal billing in the marital chain of command?

My focus has always been on struggling to maintain control—my control—rather than what the issue actually is: trusting myself to God. My sense of personal safe-ness stays intact if I'm the one making decisions about my life. Relinquishing that responsibility to someone else, even someone who loves me and has my best interests at heart, makes me feel insecure.[1]

Trust is the missing element.

The biblical progression of marital submission is that the woman submits to the man, and the man submits to God. Only in that context (the husband is a believer, choosing to submit to God) will the process be fruitful.

Men don't get off the hook. Everyone is called to yield himself or herself to another authority, to answer to someone. The process of yielding—as we do daily in our cars at yield signs—involves willingly following, intentionally allowing another to take the lead. It means purposely extinguishing the burning desire to play our cards our own way, and not flaming with anger when we're trumped.

This makes sense to me when I remember my 18-month-old toddler repeatedly snatching a fork off the table and tearing around the house. She chafed against yielding to my authority and threw a screaming hissy fit when I pried the dangerous utensil from her chubby little fist; but in the end, she had to submit to my leadership for her own wellbeing. The authority system was in place to protect her, not ruin her creativity or stifle her gifts and abilities.

The real reason we submit has nothing to do with being a woman. It's because as believers, our ultimate goal is to become Christlike, and Christ exemplified willing submission to His Father by humbling Himself even to the point of death.

The truth is that when I'm submitting to my partner, I'm really submitting to God. And I intentionally use that word, "partner," because that's the key to making biblical submission work.

The submission concept finally became clear to me at my nephew's wedding. With much wheedling, whining and begging, Chuck finally took the floor with me for a slow dance. I convinced him it was simple—we just had to stand there and sway in the same direction at the same time. But suddenly everyone around us was ballroom dancing. Chuck turned to flee for his chair.

"Oh, come on. Nobody's watching us," I cajoled, raising my left hand to his shoulder and grabbing his left hand in my right. "How hard can it be?"

Well, after stomping on each other's toes, butting heads (literally and figuratively) and pushing each other around as we wrestled for the lead, we retreated to our chairs, sullen and humiliated. Dancing is a partnership that doesn't work unless one partner takes the lead and the other willingly follows. Follows—as in *submits*.

Like dancing, marriage consists of two roles: the leader and the follower. The two agree on the steps so they can move in unison to achieve their mutual goal: a beautiful harmony of expression. Otherwise, they are out of sync, stepping on each other, inflicting wounds and creating resentment.

Submitting doesn't mean that we're weak or any less capable than our husbands. It simply means we choose to let him lead the dance. It actually works to our advantage—we can relax and enjoy the ride, not worrying about the next step.

Of course, there will be times when Spouse blows it. And times when we get so frustrated, we might even tear pages from our Bibles (I don't advocate this!). But the bottom line is that God set up the family structure for a reason. Women may be smarter in some ways and quicker about fixing problems, but God's Word states that we must, in love, submit to our partner in order to keep on dancing and not end up in a heap in the corner.

*Lord of the Dance, help me to remember that
You are infinitely bigger than my husband, and that
You can and will make Your will happen through the
channels of authority You've designed.*

Faith in Action

1. What do you feel God is saying about marriage in Ephesians 5:22-33? First Peter 3:1-7? Colossians 3:18-19? (If you want to delve deeper, also read 1 Corinthians 7.)

2. How is your marriage partnership like a dance? Do you two spend more time doing the twist or the tango? Do you ever struggle with who will lead and who will follow?

3. List three practical ways you can become more in sync with your partner in your matrimonial dance.

Note

1. Special thanks to Cheryl Barber, my wise and wacky submission mentor.

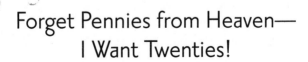

Forget Pennies from Heaven— I Want Twenties!

Money Grubbing

Marriage halves our griefs, doubles our joys, and quadruples our expenses.
OLD ENGLISH PROVERB

Don't fall in love with money. Be satisfied with what you have.
HEBREWS 13:5, *CEV*

A strange rustling noise beneath my bed woke me around 3:00 A.M. What in the world? Maybe the roaches were having a friendly game of field hockey with the dust bunnies. I rolled over and started to drift off when I heard it again, this time accompanied by a ripping sound.

I dragged myself out of bed and flipped on the light switch. Dropping to all fours, I peered under the bed until my eyes adjusted to the darkness. What I saw made my heart lurch and my mouth go dry. There was my salivating pup, cradling a large, round object between his front paws. I knew immediately what it was.

For years, I've been squirreling away a small portion of my income, supposedly as an emergency fund, but more often used for those little extras for the kids that I feel too guilty to purchase from the general family fund. For convenience, I kept the stash in an envelope buried beneath a stack of boxes under my bed.

Well, apparently my treasure had been unburied. There sat my grinning mutt, preparing to rip into my rolled-up wad of bills. The envelope had been peeled like a banana, and $300 in twenties were dripping with canine drool—my entire motherly life savings about to be devoured in a single slob- bery gulp.

It was the only time in my life I've been thankful that I'm a light sleeper!

You know, there's something funny about money. It lures us, intrigues us, controls us and absorbs us if we're not care- ful. The good part about it is that it does make us get out of bed in the morning and go to work; but the down side is, at- taining money sucks out our creative energies, often leaving only dregs for our family, like limp tea leaves in the bottom of a teacup after the world has had its fill.

I know you're thinking, "If the dang fool had kept her money in the bank, the dog would've never gotten hold of it." You're right, of course. But I learned that bad habit from Aunt EE. Remember her from "Sweet Persimmons"?

Aunt EE didn't believe in banks, so she hid money all around her house. A source of ulcers among the adult rela- tives, it delighted us kids to spot greenbacks peeking from obscure nooks and crannies, or find bags of silver dollars buried beneath the fig tree.

Immediately after Aunt EE died of heart failure, a distant cousin on EE's *other* side (not to be confused with my mother's fine, upstanding clan) locked herself in EE's house with a knife, scissors and crowbar. Emerging two days later, she left in her wake disemboweled mattresses, overturned furniture, pic- tures ripped from their frames, pried-up floorboards and a yard pitted with fresh holes. She claimed she'd found nothing, so sadly there was nothing to share with the relatives.

We were mad as wet hornets . . . because we hadn't thought of it first.

The Bible warns us not to fall in love with money, but it's incredibly hard not to, especially if you don't have any. Then money becomes like a savior, a mystical way to rise above problems and enjoy the good things of life. It's the promise of Utopia, Paradise and Shangri-La complete with bon-bons, smiling, exquisitely clad children, swimming pools, and silk blouses ruffling in the tropical breeze. Life would be like one continuous MasterCard commercial.

But this magical, fix-all place doesn't really exist. Like a vapor, it looks real until you try to grasp it.

An extremely wealthy person once told me that if you're not at peace *without* money, you'll never be at peace *with* money. Wealth tends to consume the soul, leaving a person as empty as a corn-less shuck.

God tells us to be satisfied with what we have.

I suppose that means I'll have to overlook the kitty vomit motif on the carpet a while longer and keep prayerfully laying hands on the dancing washing machine as it mambos across the floor. The kids can beg their little guts out for an upgraded electronic game, but it's not gonna happen. One day maybe I'll be able to afford better. For now, I'll focus on the wealth of blessings God has given me, and hide the carpet stains with another throw (up) rug.

Giver of all good things, help me to not get lost in the woods of discontent that border my blessings. Quench my insatiable thirst for money and help me not to focus on my wants, but trust You to provide for all my needs.

Faith in Action

1. What is your biggest dream regarding money? What is your biggest fear about money?

2. Do you ever think of money as your "ticket out"? Out of what?

3. What steps can you take to become more satisfied with what you have (see Hebrews 13:5)?

Losing the Big "L"
Winning Attitude

We are always getting ready to live, but never living.
RALPH WALDO EMERSON

*I know you inside and out, and find little to my liking. You're not
cold, you're not hot—far better to be either cold or hot! You're stale.
You're stagnant. You make me want to vomit.*
REVELATION 3:15-16, *THE MESSAGE*

When I was in high school, I was always second best. Number-
two position on the tennis team, red ribbon in the science
fair, vice president of the student body; and I finished one-
tenth of a point behind my best friend's GPA.

Playing second fiddle is frustrating. Even the tone-deaf
realize you're flat.

I couldn't actually *win* anything. I'll never forget our All
Sports Banquet in twelfth grade. It was my turn to receive
the MVP (Most Valuable Player) award for tennis. It always
went to a senior, and as the only senior on the team, I was a
shoo-in. I spent hours getting dolled up (there were football
players to impress!) and when the banquet climaxed with
the awards ceremony, my palms got sweaty, and razor-edged
butterflies ripped my stomach to shreds.

But for the first time in history, the tennis MVP trophy
went to a junior—Jumper Jones.[1] Jumper was my archenemy,

my biggest nemesis, the slim girl with the long legs who sneered at me because I couldn't beat her the entire season.

That same year, delusional friends encouraged me to run for homecoming queen. I knew, however, that Amber, the prettiest and most popular girl in the school, would run.[2] Amber could sing, too. Not that homecoming queens had to sing, but it was just the idea that she *could*. (Doesn't that just gall your bladder when the *Barbies* who have everything can sing too?)

Anyway, I was sure that dumpy Debbie (whose voice cracks like Ken in puberty) would once again be humiliated. So I didn't even try.

Far from living large, I was living lukewarm. Not hot, nearly cold. I just couldn't—or wouldn't—put out that extra effort to *achieve*.

Then at my graduation ceremony, the coup de grâce. I was given the teacher-selected, "I DARE YOU!" award for girls. What in the world was that supposed to mean? I took it as the "Most Pathetic Underachiever" award. One look at the boy who received the award was enough to tell me what I already knew. Lonnie Pile was smart, witty, multitalented and a big loser.[3] He was lazy—unmotivated to actually use any of his abilities except to some disgusting or devious end.

So I slunk across the stage to receive my plaque with a huge invisible "L" plastered to my forehead. Or so I thought at the time.

But a funny thing happened about eight years after high school. I had kids. My viewpoint began to change. The passive little girl who'd always accepted her lot in life as second best got, well, fired up. I wanted—no, demanded—the very best for my kids. I intended for them to reach for the stars and be all they could possibly be.

Second best wasn't good enough. Not for them, and not for me.

Philippians 4:13 lit a spark that blazed in my soul. "I can do all things through Him who strengthens me" (*NLT*). Was it true? The verse didn't say *some* things, it said *all* things. I finally had a creed, a powerful truth to cling to, the spur I needed to give me confidence to lead by example in going for the gold in pursuing my life goals and encouraging my children that they could, too. Silver just wouldn't cut it when it came to using every last God-given gift and ability to His glory.

"Okay," I challenged life. "Go ahead and dare me. I accept that dare!"

I'd been blessed with a natural affinity for the written word and always dreamed of being a writer. So I dared to try. I now write Christian magazine articles and books with the single goal of expanding God's kingdom.

My kids dared, too. The Lord gave my son a memory like a steel trap; he recently graduated with his MBA and helps people climb out of financial trouble. My daughter's gifts are sensitivity and compassion; she makes a huge difference in the lives of countless people by daring to reach out with tangible reminders of God's intimate love.

I wish I'd kept my I DARE YOU plaque. I would hang it in my office as a daily reminder that living lukewarm only creates nausea.

*Jehovah-Jireh (God, our Provider), thanks for
not spewing my lazy, lukewarm self out of Your mouth,
but firing up my heart to a toasty intensity that
I daresay is neither stagnant nor stale.*

Faith in Action

1. Can you remember a time in your life when you thought of yourself as a loser? What caused you to see yourself that way?

2. Has there been a time when your child struggled with feeling like a loser?

3. How can Philippians 4:13 give you—and your children—confidence to accept life's dare and aggressively pursue the dreams God has planted in your heart?

Notes

1. FYI: Jumper disappeared into tennis obscurity after high school, while *I* (can you feel my humility?) am still swinging a racquet 30 years later.
2. Amber, ex-homecoming queen, married at 18 and started plunking out babies. Now a size-4 grandmother who looks like Workout Barbie's older sister, she recently cut a CD.
3. Lonnie Pile, a Christian husband and father of two, dared to become a hugely successful radio personality.

Ode to Daddy

Godly Parenting

When you get to the end of your rope,
you'll find God waiting with a ladder.
A VERY TIRED PARENT

Fathers, do not exasperate your children; instead,
bring them up in the training and instruction of the Lord.
EPHESIANS 6:4, *NIV*

It's time again for Daddy's haircut, a father-daughter ritual that dates back to my teen years when I was the primary hairdresser in my little world. It wasn't a task I enjoyed then, only an inconvenience to be tolerated.

Now, as Daddy sits serenely on a stool beneath the spreading oaks in the front yard, I see my aging father in a different light. His posture, once tall and straight, is now hunched. The thick black hair gracing the memories of my youth is now thinning and mottled with gray.

As I drape the towel around his shoulders, my mind returns to the daddy of my childhood.

He was the protective giant I could always run to in times of doubt or fear. Before his name stopped echoing through the darkened house after another of my terrifying nightmares, Daddy was there. Never scolding, he'd pat my back as he folded his large frame into my little bed, soothing me back to sleep by his comforting presence.

Before daybreak, I'd follow him into the bathroom as he shaved and readied himself for work. He'd carefully spread a thick bath towel on the cold bathroom floor so I could curl up around his feet and listen to endless tales of knights and ladies, unwise home-building pigs and a cinder girl who found happiness ever after.

The memories melt away and I smile as Daddy waits patiently for me to begin his haircut.

Patience and dignity were always his way—very different from his fiery wife and two temperamental daughters. He was a calming balance, speaking little but saying much through his steadfast love for us and his Lord. He took us to church each time the doors opened and led our family in Bible reading and prayer every night.

Daddy taught me how to *feel* God on long walks through the woods on hot summer afternoons, or in the stillness of crisp fall nights. Words weren't necessary. I'd slip my hand in his and we'd worship our Creator together.

I gather a tuft of Daddy's hair between my fingers and begin to cut, the rich texture of the strands brings a warm feeling of intimacy with this man, a relationship like no other in my life . . . a daughter's love for her papa. Even through those turbulent adolescent years when I viewed my parents through the haze of rebellion, I knew beyond a doubt that he loved me and would always stand behind me.

We continue Daddy's haircut in companionable silence, with an occasional comment about the remarkable quantity of hair gone underground and sprigging from his ears, nose and everywhere but his scalp. We both grin.

Daddy's wry sense of humor is a trait I thankfully inherited. He managed to see humor in many awkward situations, making life's testy moments not only bearable but also sometimes downright hilarious.

Like the time I was too sick for school, so Daddy took me to work with him. He was a hospital laboratory technician, and as a curious eight-year-old, I loved to watch vials of blood spinning in the centrifuge or peer through the microscope at "squigglers" on glass slides. Even more fun was peeking through the holes in the large metal container stored in the lab refrigerator. It held several dozen toads used for medical tests, and I liked to poke my finger through the holes and watch them hop around.

While Daddy was out delivering a lab report, I started wondering what it would feel like to actually hold one of those squishy amphibians. I carefully slid the metal tray onto the floor. As I lifted the heavy lid, every last toad leapt in unison out of their prison and liberated themselves down the hallways and throughout the hospital.

While the other hospital personnel shouted, grumbled or glared at me in sheer exasperation, Daddy quietly shook his head and turned away with a smile tugging at his lips. I knew that I'd committed a terrible sin, but I also knew that I would be forgiven and loved no less by the only one who really counted.

Just like my heavenly Father forgives and loves me today.

Leaning close to trim Daddy's incorrigible cowlick, my eyes fill with tears as my heart is filled with love for this gentle man who lived out his conviction that God and his family were above all else in life. Future family generations may not realize the origins of their deep roots of faith, but I know. *He* was the one planting seeds in the fertile soil of our spirits, quietly showing us how to live and love and worship.

I shake out the towel and gather my haircutting tools. Daddy softly groans as he rises, his arthritic joints protesting mercilessly. I tenderly smile as I slip my hand into his for the journey home.

Heavenly Father, I am humbled by the blessing of a loving earthly father, but some of my sisters look to You as their only example of a true father. Thank You, Papa God, for filling that void.

Faith in Action

1. What characteristics of your father do you carry with you today?

2. According to Psalm 68:5, God is a father of the fatherless. Some of our sisters have only their heavenly Father as an example of a true father. If you are one of these, what attributes has Papa God (Abba Father) brought into your life that have helped mold you into the woman you are today?

3. Think of three ways you can intertwine the love of your heavenly Father with the lives of your children likes cords of a strong rope.

Beauty Is the Beast
Self-Worth

*Laughter is to joy like a 50% OFF sign is to shopping.
A flame is sparked deep in our innards to seek more, more, more!*
DEBORA M. COTY

*Charm is deceptive, and beauty is fleeting;
but a woman who fears the LORD is to be praised.*

PROVERBS 31:30, *NIV*

If you're like me, you have three halves to your closet: the skinny half (those teensy sizes from the glory days, now wreathed in spider webs); the regular half (the majority of your wardrobe); the fat half (garments whose massive bulk makes them appear more numerous than they are).

The skinny clothes are those adorable outfits you can't bear to part with because you *know* one day you'll shimmy into them again. The regulars are the tried and true, the wardrobe you live in daily. The fat clothes are insurance; you only touch them on those horrible days when bloated bunnies burrow in your drawers, or the previous week's cheesecake catches up with your caboose.

It's the dark ages indeed when you must tap into the rotunda clothes so often that they gradually migrate into the regulars and you even begin adding to their number.

Heavy sigh.

I knew I was in trouble when I couldn't zip any of my nice pantsuits and I had an upcoming speaking engagement. What to do? No time to shop (too depressing anyway). The answer to my problem presented itself with the daily mail. Ah ha! A mail order catalog!

I quickly spotted a dignified but elastically functional (that means bending over won't pinch the waist rolls or produce a wedgie up to the eyeballs) pantsuit that was a lovely shade of mauve. Perfect. I'd look like a blushing petunia. I immediately ordered one a size larger than usual. Not because I'm bigger, of course, but because the fabric looked like a high shrink risk (they're *all* high shrink risks when they're double digits!).

With only days to spare, the outfit arrived and I hastened to try it on. Wait—what was this? There were three buttons and three buttonholes on the right side of the double-breasted jacket, but only two buttonholes for the three buttons on the left. This unfortunate omission left the jacket gaping open directly over my left bosom.

Now this may be an ingenious fashion statement for Madonna, Janet or Britney, but not for a mega mama speaking to a group of hungry Kiwanis.

Indignant, I called the catalog company.

"Yes ma'am? How may I help you?"

"Why, you can send me a buttonhole!"

"Excuse me? Your item is missing a button?"

"A button*hole*! My jacket has three buttons and two buttonholes. You forgot my buttonhole!"

"Uh, ma'am, would that be a double-breasted jacket?"

"Yes, it would."

"Well, that's the way they come."

"What? That can't be right." I flipped to the catalog picture, and sure enough, while all the other buttons harmonized with their holes, the pencil-thin model's top left button was performing a solo. On her it was hardly noticeable. On me, it would be a ticket to the slammer for indecent exposure.

A local seamstress graciously zapped the gap with a brand new buttonhole.

That story reminds me of my friend Ellen, who lost 90 pounds. Ellen was pleased with her new body except for one thing. Her breasts, once ripe melons, now sagged to her knees like deflated blimps. She had to scoop them up and tuck them into her bra each morning, arranging and plumping them to form cleavage. Not unlike readying feather pillows for a good night's sleep.

I recall feeling awed about my boobage when nursing my baby while talking on the phone and fixing dinner simultaneously. They really are amazing—breasts—as they stretch like rubber bands and assume any position necessary to do their jobs, even wrapping themselves around pot handles when necessary. I think we should organize a Boob Appreciation Day (B.A.D.). We could strap on fake cow udders and fasten balloons all over our bodies.

The Bible reminds us that beauty is fleeting—here today, gone tomorrow. Beauty is a beastly boss, but we find ourselves yielding to its relentless siege on our self-esteem. Pressure begins early. As new mothers, the compliment we yearn to hear is, "My, what a beautiful baby!"

We'll love our children no matter how they look, but somehow beauty and affirmation of worth have become intertwined. Through society's warped standards we've inadvertently allowed the value of ourselves and our children to become dependent on appearance; or worse, dependent on other people's response to our appearance.

I'll never forget cowering on the high dive at the public pool as a 12-year-old, self-conscious about my changing body and feeling exposed to the world in my bathing suit. Afraid to jump, I backed away from the edge, crowding the older girl in line behind me.

"Go on, jump!" she snapped. I hesitated, trembling.

She shook her head with contempt. "You shouldn't be up here. You're chicken. You're fat. And you're *ugly*."

I jumped. It was the only way to hide the tears.

God of mercy and grace, fill me with inner beauty
that comes from Your unconditional love. Teach me that
to You, I am beautiful, beloved and of great worth.
All other measuring sticks are just wood.

Faith in Action

1. What does Proverbs 31:30 mean: "a woman who fears the LORD is to be praised" (*NIV*)? In what sense is the word "fear" used here?

2. Why does the Bible say, "Charm is deceptive"? What do you think this implies about our basic human nature?

3. What do you think are the underlying reasons we allow society's beastly beauty norms to control our self-esteem and sense of personal worth?

Becoming God's Garbage Girl
Loving Your Neighbor

It's never too late to be what you might have been.
GEORGE ELIOT

Dear friends, since God so loved us, we also ought to love one another.
1 JOHN 4:11, *NIV*

I can't believe it! There it is again—my neighbor's trash, blowing onto my lawn for the umpteenth time, invading *my* space, becoming *my* eyesore. For many months, this problem has been a burr under my saddle . . . a worm in my salad . . . a bee at my picnic. With the regularity of a grandpa on Grape Nuts, each trash pick-up day I can count on bits and pieces of fallen refuse finding its way into my yard.

Maybe it's just the way the wind blows. Perhaps it's the position of my house in the cul-de-sac. I'm beginning to think it's the devil having a good chuckle about getting under my skin again. He's quite skilled at finding just the right nail to hammer in order to drive a wedge between me and my neighbors.

These are people who *must* see their loose trash lying beside their cans when they go out to retrieve them, but they don't bend down and pick it up. One night, after a grease-stained pizza box had languished in the gutter all day, I shoved it back into their yard with my foot so there would be no doubt who "owned" the trash. The next morning, their newspaper was lying within two feet of the pizza box, but by the end of the day, the newspaper was gone while the box was back in the cul-de-sac, heading toward my house.

I finally realized that gnashing my teeth and muttering under my breath was not the best way to witness to these people. It doesn't really speak well of God's love in your heart when you're tossing rotten apple cores over their fence. "Be careful how you live among your unbelieving neighbors" (1 Peter 2:12, *NLT*).

My friend Elaine was having a similar problem with her neighbor, and in order to keep the peace, she came to a very wise conclusion: *Sometimes you just have to become God's garbage girl.*

So, is becoming God's garbage girl a scriptural principle? My answer was found in Leviticus 19:18: "Love your neighbor as yourself. I am the LORD" (*NIV*). Well, I guess that's pretty plain—especially God's signature at the end, emphasizing His authority for issuing this directive (in case I missed it).

Okay, so how do I love my neighbors on a day-by-day, trash-on-my-driveway basis? Changing my perspective seems to be first in line. If I can see them through God's eyes—through His filter of compassion—perhaps love will eventually follow.

My heart did soften a smidge when I learned the husband is in chronic pain due to multiple back surgeries and the wife works two jobs to make ends meet. Maybe that is why picking up garbage is not a priority for her and is impossible for him.

The picture is becoming clearer now. God gave me a strong back and agile fingers so that I can serve these needy people in a unique ministry—as their trash picker-upper. I can do that. I *want* to do it. In fact, I think I'll go out right now and remove that hamburger wrapper that's been tangled in their shrubbery for weeks.

Maybe instead of sharing apple cores, I'll share a freshly baked apple pie!

*Love Incarnate, help me see my neighbors
through Your compassionate eyes. And remind me
to keep my apple cores to myself.*

Faith in Action

1. Do you have a neighbor (or an acquaintance, not necessarily physically next door) who consistently gets under your skin? In what way?

2. Have you ever considered praying for your annoying neighbor?

3. Take a few minutes to mull over 1 John 4:11 and ask God to give you a glimpse of your neighbor through the same compassionate eyes by which He sees you.

Poppies from Poopies
Rejection

If evolution really works, how come mothers only have two hands?
MILTON BERLE

You, the LORD God, keep my lamp burning and turn darkness to light.
PSALM 18:28, *CEV*

I played on an adult tennis team for three years, and although I skipped drinks with the girls on Friday nights, I developed solid friendships with my nine teammates. Or so I thought.

Then came the skiing accident in the Canadian Rockies that ripped my knee ligaments into spaghetti. I received a few cards from the girls and admonishment to get well soon when I hobbled on my crutches to cheer them on in their matches. Mourning my wretched loss, I couldn't wait to get back on the court. I was sure my friends felt the same way.

Three surgeries, painful rehab and 14 months later, I was eager to return to my place on the team. But there was no longer a place for me. No phone calls. No friendly emails. When a position came open, it was quickly filled with someone else.

"Why?" I asked.

"Because you're not good enough to be one of us anymore," I was told.

Rejection. We get it from all sides. Even more heartbreaking, our children experience rejection as a normal part of childhood. She's the wrong sex for the *Boys Only* club. He's too clumsy to make the team. Her clothes don't have the right designer labels to fit in with the group.

Moms get it, too. You're not invited to the cookware party, although your best friend is. That wimpy minivan is shunned by the Hummer crowd. You're snubbed as the stick-in-the-mud mom who doesn't let her preteen go to mixed sleepovers. Though you know in your head that rejection is unjust and doesn't alter your worth before God, the light in your heart still feels extinguished. Rejection threatens to douse the flame of your internal lamp. Only God can keep the wick glowing when the fire all but burns out.

As a country girl, I try to view rejection as farmers view cow patties: an inevitable inconvenience. Not a barricade. Not an impassable obstruction. Just an inconvenience. So shovel them aside, step over the piles and keep going. The Lord specializes in making positives from negatives. In His garden of life, cow patty fertilizer produces glorious flower blossoms. He creates poppies from poopies!

As harsh as it sounds, rejection is often an essential part of God's plan for us.

I once submitted a book proposal to a prominent publishing house. I was thrilled when an editor asked to see the complete manuscript. During the following three months, my hopes were built higher and higher as my manuscript climbed the ladder of editors toward final rung of approval for publication.

In the eleventh hour, at the final editorial meeting, a decision was made. You guessed it: Rejection. My hopes and dreams crashed and burned.

Two days later, I managed to quit wallowing in my despair long enough to email the editor a brief note thanking her for her encouragement throughout the ill-fated journey and asked what went wrong. She responded that it had nothing to do with the quality of my work; because of two similar books in their line, the company decided not to publish mine.

Bummer.

Before I could reply, I received another email from that same editor asking if I'd be interested in a new project. They were looking for a writer with, well, just my flair.

Knock me over with a feather! Out of the darkness of rejection comes joy with the radiant morning!

God's making poppies from poopies again!

Light of the Morning [see 2 Samuel 23:4], keep my lamp burning through the black night of rejection until You bring joyful hope with the morning. Help me to be sensitive about unintentionally inflicting the pain of rejection on others.

Faith in Action

1. Describe a time during the last month in which you felt rejected. How can Psalm 30:5 help you resolve your hurt?

2. Now reflect on a recent time when your child faced rejection. How can you share hope for "joy in the morning" with him or her?

3. Can you recall two incidences of rejection in your life when you later realized that God was creating poppies from poopies? (In other words, rejection was essential for God's plan for you to unfold in the way that it did.) Resolve to remember this lesson for future rejections!

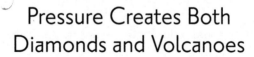

Pressure Creates Both Diamonds and Volcanoes

Peer Pressure

In laugh or cry situations, thanks, Lord, for helping me choose to laugh!
DEBORA M. COTY

Be careful to do what the LORD your God has commanded you;
do not turn aside to the right or to the left.
DEUTERONOMY 5:32, *NIV*

My first-grade daughter, nicknamed Cricket, received an invitation to play at a friend's house after school. I'd met Jessie and her mom at school functions and they seemed nice enough. I knew that Jessie's family attended the church that sponsored the Christian school my kids attended, so I agreed to pick up Cricket in time for dinner.

Imagine my surprise when my innocent little girl, toting her Cinderella book bag, climbed in my car singing, "I had . . . the time of my li-i-ife . . . and I owe it all to you-ou-ou-ou-ou."

My protective mother alarm clanged. "Where did you hear that?"

"Jessie's mom let us pick a video, and Jessie picked *Dirty Dancing*. She's seen it a bunch, but I never have. Why don't you let us watch cool stuff like that?"

"Because you're six!" I shouted over the voice in my head blaring, *Red Alert! Red Alert!*

Peer pressure and the world's influence manage to creep in no matter how careful we are as parents. That's why it's so important to instill God's principles into our children from the day they are born. In this fast-moving, media-driven culture, they must rely on personal resources for wise decision-making even more than our generation did.

Those resources *must* include unconditional open doors to Mom for help with difficult choices.

As a senior in high school, Cricket was befriended by Holly, a bubbly girl who quickly became a part of her inner circle. Cricket's friends became Holly's friends. Holly spent so much time at our house that we began to think of her as our other daughter. Because she was from a blue-collar immigrant family, we happily paid Holly's way at restaurants, ballgames, amusement parks and even a vacation with our family.

I began wondering how she could afford the sleek black sports car she drove, the cell phone she was never without and the designer clothes she brought home from the mall. Holly had an after-school waitress job, but something didn't add up. I asked if her parents helped pay her bills, and she replied, "Oh, I have plenty of help getting what I need."

About three months into the school year, I noticed money periodically missing from my wallet. Cricket tearfully misplaced her $50 Christmas fund. A school friend reported her paycheck was stolen from her wallet during class. Yet another friend couldn't find $100 she had hidden beneath her mattress in her bedroom.

One afternoon, Cricket came home hot and sweaty from basketball practice with Holly in tow. Cricket went to the bathroom to shower, leaving Holly watching television in the family room. After turning on the water, Cricket realized that she'd forgotten her comb, so she slipped back to her bedroom.

There was Holly, bending over Cricket's opened purse.

"What are you doing?" Cricket asked, a horrible dark cloud filling her heart.

"Oh, I'm just looking for an earring I dropped," Holly casually replied. "Listen, I've got to go for a few hours, but I'll be back for dinner; your mom's making my favorite casserole." Holly headed for the door, leaving Cricket thoroughly shaken.

Ten minutes later, a sobbing Cricket interrupted my piano lesson. "Mom, the only $20 bill I had in my purse is gone. If she'd asked for it, I would have given it to her. But Holly stole it. What should I do?"

Cricket was distraught; together we confronted Holly. She vehemently denied guilt, but a police investigation revealed she'd stolen over $2,500 in cash and forged checks to pay for the trappings peer pressure deemed necessary. She'd *used* Cricket, our family and trusting friends in her attempt to blend in, to look like "everybody else," to feel accepted.

How do we ensure that our children don't turn to the right or to the left of God's righteous path and yield to peer pressure?

Sadly, there's no formula to guarantee that our kids will stay the course. But if we commit to developing cornerstones of conviction in our children's hearts—the *only* reason to say no during the bombardment of peer pressure—we stand a fighting chance.

What are these defensive basics to build in our kids, brick by brick, wall by wall?

1. A strong discernment of right and wrong based on God's Word. "Do not let this Book of the Law depart from your mouth; meditate on it day and night, so that you may be careful to do everything written in it . . . Be strong and courageous . . . for the LORD your God will be with you wherever you go" (Joshua 1:8-9, *NIV*).

2. A healthy respect for God . . . and Mom. "Now fear the LORD and serve him with all faithfulness" (Joshua 24:14, *NIV*). "The rod of correction imparts wisdom, but a child left to himself disgraces his mother" (Proverbs 29:15, *NIV*).

Father God, the only way my kids can withstand peer pressure is through a relationship with You. I ask, Lord, that You draw them unto Yourself so that their own convictions would take root and grow out of their love for You. In the meantime, my rod of correction will have to fill the gap.

Faith in Action

1. How does peer pressure affect your children on a daily basis?

2. Do your children feel that the door is unconditionally open to seek your help for difficult choices? If not, what are three steps you can take to prop that door open for good?

3. Discuss creative ways you can apply Joshua 1:8-9 and 24:14 to help build cornerstones of conviction in your child's heart.

Dashing the Joy-Sucking Dully-Funks

Triumphant Humor

Wrinkles should merely indicate where smiles have been.
MARK TWAIN

A joyful heart is good medicine.
PROVERBS 17:22, *NASB*

God, the original humor designer, doesn't want His children to wallow in the doldrums and dully-funks. I think He takes delight in the innocence of chuckles, snickers and guffaws and probably smiles right along with us when His masterpiece of creation—pure, belly-tickling laughter—is elicited; like my mother's comment when her youngest granddaughter was showing off her brand-new Bible. "Oh, look! You have the New Intestinal Version!" (I couldn't help but ask if it was the large or small intestinal version!)

My son's first grade Sunday school teacher was telling the story of Naaman the leper in the fifth chapter of 2 Kings. He was healed after dunking himself in the Jordan River seven times according to the prophet Elisha's instructions. Near the end of class, the teacher noticed that six-year-old Matthew was staring out the window daydreaming and asked him to recap the story.

Ever the NBA fan, Matthew never missed a beat (or a dribble). "Eli Shaw—I reckon he was the coach—told Michael Jordan to slam-dunk seven times beside the river to whip them Leopards."

Other insightful bits of biblical knowledge we've learned from children include Noah's floating arcade landing on Mt. Thermostat; God writing on aspirin tablets to give Moses the ten commandos up on Mount Cyanide; and the hysterical (historical) figure of Solar-man (Solomon), who kept very busy with 700 wives and 300 porcupines.

Oh, a very good question for you to ponder on a rainy day: Did Noah take a pair of termites on the ark?

Our youth group was visited by a teenager who'd never been to church or read the Bible. During a game of Bible trivia, he was confronted with the question: *What did Peter do when the cock crowed for the third time?* After brief reflection on his personal experience with "alarm-cocks," the resourceful teen answered, "He dragged his lazy kiester out of bed."

Another teen thought a concubine was the machine that harvests corn on a farm.

Are you grinning yet?

A friend told me of the time she was sitting in church directly behind the minister's wife, a generously endowed, large-busted woman. The preacher was deep into his sermon on the wonders of heaven when he glanced at his adoring wife. "I just can't wait to walk through God's flower garden on that day of rejoicing," he said, dramatically kneeling on one knee and cupping his hands. "I can't wait to bend down among those fragrant buds and hold one of those beautiful bosoms in my hand."

Oops. Can you say "blossom," as in the rose-colored face of the minister's wife?

Now, don't you feel like you've had a dose of good medicine to jumpstart your day on a joyful note? Never forget the admonition of the most gravity-challenged prophet in the Bible, Knee-high-miah (Nehemiah): "The joy of the Lord is your strength."

> *Lord of heaven and mirth, creator of goony birds,*
> *walking catfish and toe jam, fill us with your*
> *joy and strength; open our eyes to see your levity*
> *around us, especially when our spirits are weighted*
> *down by the joy-sucking dully-funks.*

Faith in Action

1. When was the last time you could honestly sing, "I've got the joy, joy, joy, joy down in my heart"? What is preventing you from singing it today?

2. List three ways you can (and will) share joy with your children. (Examples: bake brownies together and take turns licking the mixing bowl, play an old-fashioned board game, walk in the rain holding hands build a snowman or a sand castle together, pick wild flowers.)

3. Do something before nightfall *today* to elicit a big ol' juicy belly laugh from your child; bet you'll join in too!

Acknowledgments

Many thanks to WordServe Literary Group's Greg Johnson for his faith in this book. Much gratitude is also extended to Kim Bangs and the gracious folks at Regal Books for—as the old Abba song goes—taking a chance on me. Hugs and kisses to my terrific family for providing story fodder with love. And eternal gratitude to Papa God for His everyday amazing grace notes.

Visit with the Author

You can learn more about Debora M. Coty at her website, www.DeboraCoty.com. Deb would love to share God's levity of love with your group, or just bust a few dully-funks and chew the chocolate with you at gracenotes@deboracoty.com. Look for these faith-inspiring books by Debora M. Coty:

The Distant Shore
Young adult historical fiction inspired by the
true story of a young girl's journey of faith on
Florida's remote, untamed Merritt Island, in 1904.
Because love is never too lost or too late.

Billowing Sails
In this sequel to *The Distant Shore,* Emma-Lee
continues her quest for belonging against a
backdrop of romance, rocky family relationships
and pre-World War I international espionage.
Some dreams should never end.

Grit for the Oyster:
250 Pearls of Wisdom for Aspiring Writers
Chock-full of writing tips from top
Christian authors, poets, editors and agents,
this devotional style book will inspire and
encourage writers on every level.